FOUR PILLARS
OF JUNGIAN
PSYCHOANALYSIS

Murray Stein

CHIRON PUBLICATIONS • ASHEVILLE, NORTH CAROLINA

© 2022 by Chiron Publications. All rights reserved. No part of this publication may be reproduced, stored in a retrieval system, or transmitted, in any form by any means, electronic, mechanical, photocopying, recording, or otherwise, without the prior written permission of the publisher, Chiron Publications, P.O. Box 19690, Asheville, N.C. 28815-1690.

www.ChironPublications.com

Front cover painting by Diane Stanley©
Interior and cover design by Danijela Mijailovic
Printed primarily in the United States of America.

ISBN 978-1-68503-025-4 paperback
ISBN 978-1-68503-026-1 hardcover
ISBN 978-1-68503-027-8 electronic
ISBN 978-1-68503-028-5 limited edition paperback

Library of Congress Cataloging-in-Publication Data
Pending

Table of Contents

A Brief Introduction

Jungian psychoanalysis is a type of psychotherapy. There are many approaches to psychotherapy on offer to people seeking psychological help today, and people often wonder about the differences among them and whether these differences really matter as far as clinical treatment is concerned. Outcome studies generally suggest that the quality of the therapist is more important than the theory being used. Yet people are curious, and I believe the theory does make a difference because it guides the work of the therapist, whether the client realizes it or not.

It is in response to this question that I have drafted these four chapters on Jungian psychoanalysis. The question I'm addressing is: What makes the Jungian approach unique and different from the others? I've reflected on this quite a lot and discussed it with colleagues in my field and in other schools, and I've read psychotherapeutic literature widely for many years now. I've boiled it down to four essential features that, when combined, are central to the Jungian approach and set it apart from the others. They are what I am calling the Four Pillars of Jungian Psycho-analysis. I will elaborate on each of them in turn in the following chapters, but here I offer a brief overview for the reader's initial orientation.

The first pillar consists of a way of thinking about psychological development. In the Jungian school, this is called individuation. The concept of individuation offers a map for tracking a lifelong developmental process. A second distinguishing feature is a particular way of understanding the therapeutic relationship. For this we generally use the terms transference and countertransference. These terms originate in the psychoanalytic voca-bulary that Jung constructed with Freud in his apprenticeship as a psychoanalyst, but we have a significantly different way of thinking about it from the Freudian and other perspectives. This relationship implies a deeper and more complex connection between analyst and client than the obvious one typically referred to as a therapeutic relationship. This subject comprises the second pillar.

The third major feature that distinguishes a Jungian approach is that we work intensively with the client's dreams. Dreams are not only welcome in analysis; they are actively sought for and employed as doorways to the unconscious. Dreams are considered essential in Jungian psychoanalysis for going forward in the analytic process. How we think about dreams, how we interpret them and work with them, is the focus of the third pillar.

The fourth pillar, active imagination, is unique to Jungian psychoanalysis. This method involves an attempt to engage with the processes of the unconscious directly. It is related to but significantly different from working with dreams and is used for specific purposes within the context of Jungian psychotherapy.

It is the combination of these four elements that distinguishes Jungian psychoanalysis from other forms of psychotherapy. The trained Jungian psychoanalyst will be familiar with them and use them as appropriate with individual clients. Each analysis is unique, and there are no recipes for analysis, but these are methods that may be used.

Pillar One

The Individuation Process

Jungian psychoanalysts are trained to refrain from using "techniques" or "recipes" in their clinical work with patients. They are encouraged by their teachers to enter every session fresh and with an open mind—welcoming the conscious and unconscious material of the client in whatever shape and form it appears—working in the immediacy of the moment face-to-face in an interactive, dynamic process. "Leave your theories and techniques at the door when you enter the consulting room!" was the Master's advice. Jungian psychoanalysts generally do not sit behind their patients and are not silent in sessions. They tend to be available and accessible; their personalities are out there on display. But, one has to admit, the analyst has a clinical perspective, and it is quite firmly fixed in mind. In the back of the analyst's mind, there is a guidance system operating based on a road map of psychological development, a lifelong process called *individuation*.

Analysts might not ever say anything to a patient about this perspective, but in the back of their minds, they are making an evaluation and a type of judgment (diagnosis) based on it. The theory of individuation elaborates a developmental program that is considered normative for people cross-culturally and more or less without exception. Jung speaks of it as archetypal, which means universally applicable for human beings as we know them. The map of individuation tells us what it is to be a human personality and informs us about the various stages of development in the course of a lifetime. It tells us what to expect as a personality develops to the maximum potential. In making an evolving assessment of individuation as achieved in specific cases, the Jungian analyst is continuously asking: "Where is this person located on the path of individuation, and what is the next step?" For this, chronological age is an important consideration. If a person is 45 years old, one has certain expectations for where that person would be normatively in their psychological development; if the person is 21 years old, those expectations are different. If the person is 75 years old, it is quite different again.

In this chapter, I want to indicate something of what that road map looks like and to speak of what is operating in the back of the mind of Jungian analysts as they assess the level of psychological development of the person sitting in front of them.

Jung is generally recognized as the first major full life-span psychological theorist. This means consideration of a psychological development process that continues through the whole course of a lifetime. Jung gave this developmental process a name—*individuation*. The basic idea behind individuation is simple. Throughout your lifetime, you become what you potentially are at the beginning. In other words, individuation is the realization of a potential self that begins its existence in the mother's womb and ends at death at whatever age has been achieved. This process of fully becoming your innate self takes an amount of time, and it proceeds through several stages.

The idea is that we come into the world as a self that is not developed and needs time to reveal a distinct individual personality. Sometimes this is called the acorn theory of psychological development. An acorn is a seed of an oak tree, and if you put it into the ground and give it time and water it, it will grow over the course of several years into a tree. The magnificent oak tree eventually becomes fully developed with great branches reaching upward toward the heavens and deep roots going far down into the earth.

The total image of the oak tree is a picture of the completed individuation process. The whole tree is contained potentially in the seed, but if you cut the acorn open you will not see a tiny version of the giant tree it will become. You only find the germ, the genetic material that in time will give this tree its distinctive shape and character.

We come into the world as a self, but it is potential. We can call this the germ seed of the self to come. In alchemical language, this is the "*prima materia*," the basic matrix that contains all that is needed in the process that will eventually become the "*lapis philosophorum.*" It will take a period of time, in fact many years, for the full personality to become fully manifest. But the original self contains all the potential, and it will unfold and develop in a particular time and place, in a particular individual and family and culture. The self is both general in that it is made up of the same material for everyone and unique in that it is a particular combination of general materials (the archetypes) and implanted in a unique body in a specific time and place. The specific and relative are backed up by the universal and absolute.

In Jungian psychology, the development of the unique and specific ego and its surrounding consciousness, as well as persona identity, represent just the beginning of the full development of the self. The self is a transcendent psychological factor in that it includes all aspects of the personality, conscious and unconscious. Some schools of psychotherapy focus on the development of ego structures and persona identity ("adjustment"). This is an important part of the individuation process as a whole, but it is not all of it. Sometimes Jung would write about individuation as becoming *what* you are, and not only *who* you are. *Who* refers to your conscious identity, but *what* is the totality of the self, the conscious and the unconscious aspects combined. A basic axiom of Jungian psychology is that "the self" is supraordinate to "the ego" and that the ego is only a part of the whole self, albeit an absolutely essential part.

Full individuation is a developmental goal, but it is not fully achievable and realizable within a single lifetime. You might wonder why that is the case? Why can't we reach the final goal of the individuation process—in other words, realization of the self completely? It is because our consciousness is not big enough to integrate the whole self. We can only partially integrate what the self fully represents. Certain aspects of the self, even after a long development of individuation, remain unconscious, beyond the reach of consciousness. The self as a whole is made up of many archetypal potentials, but an individual can realize only a few of these possibilities. An individual is a specific combination of these many archetypal possibilities. That specific combination is what the individual is responsible for realizing and manifesting as their personal life history.

Jung argued that individuation is an archetypal process with a goal. When we say that it's archetypal, we mean that it's like an instinct and it belongs to everyone: All human beings have within themselves this drive to realize an individuation process. Some people achieve a higher level of individuation than others, but this is not necessarily because they have a stronger individuation drive active within them. It's that they have consciously cooperated with this process in their lives and helped it to achieve its realization. For some people, their individuation process is limited or blocked because of lack of resources, because of traumas, or because of insurmountable cultural barriers and obstacles. Their individuation cannot be fully realized because of these factors that block and hold them back. Moreover, individuation is hard work. It takes courage and requires a lot of energy. Some people are just afraid, or lazy, or not motivated enough to assist the unconscious in the pursuit of individuation.

I will now discuss several discernable stages of the individuation process.

Jung himself divided the life span into two major stages or phases—the first half of life and the second.[1] He says life is like the journey of the

---

[1] C.G. Jung, "The Stages of Life."

sun: It rises in the east, reaches an apex at noon, and then goes down in the west and disappears in the evening. Similarly, our life begins in the darkness of the womb, emerges into the light, and rises to its zenith, then declines and finally disappears in the darkness of the tomb. From womb to tomb, that is the life span. The biblical life span was set at four score and ten, i.e., 70, but if you live in a modern culture today the average life expectancy is in the range of 80-90 years. So, the first half of life would be between 35 and 45 years, the second half of life until maybe 80 or 90+. In fact, today many people are living well and productively into their mid to late 90s, so they would have the opportunity to enjoy a considerably long second half of life.

Erich Neumann, arguably Jung's most brilliant student, made some further differentiations.[2] He divided the first half of life into two parts: The first part is "the mother stage," and the second part "the father stage." The mother stage begins in the mother's womb and continues until approximately the age of 12. Traditionally around that age, there's an initiation into adulthood, which is dominated by the father. The father stage begins around 12 and continues until midlife—around 40, typically. The second half of life is the stage of the individual. Each of these stages is dominated by a figure:

---

[2] E. Neumann, *The Origins and History of Consciousness*.

mother, father, individual. These figures are symbolic: *Mother* is the symbol for a particular atmosphere or attitude that applies to the life of childhood; *father* is a symbol of an atmosphere or an attitude that begins in adolescence and continues until the midlife period; *individual* is a symbol for an internal locus of control during this stage of life. During the first stage, the "mother principle" rules and is the reference point for the individuation process. In the second phase, the "father principle" rules and is the point of reference for the individuation process. These figures represent authority. In the first stage, the mother is the authority figure, and in the second stage, the father is the authority figure. In the third stage, the self is the authority figure.

The first drawing below represents the life span, beginning with birth (B, left side) and ending with death (D, right side). This resembles the sun traveling across the heavens, a metaphor

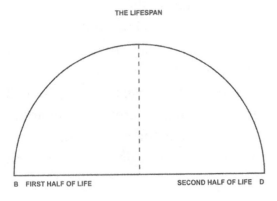

Diagram 1

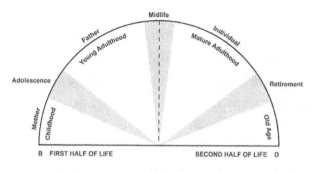

FULL LIFESPAN PSYCHOLOGICAL DEVELOPMENT (INDIVIDUATION)

Diagram 2

used by Jung to describe the life span of the individual. In his lecture on "The Stages of Life," Jung becomes poetical in his depiction of the course of life, although he also apologizes for the "lame" simile.[3]

These two halves of life can be further differentiated into several stages or phases, as shown in the second diagram above, which also includes transitional periods between the stages (diagram 2). Individuation begins in a fetus, enters the outer world at birth, moves through infancy and childhood to adolescence, which is a transitional time until early adulthood is attained. At midlife, there is another transitional period, when a person moves from early adulthood into mature adulthood. Each of these transition periods, which tend to be emotionally turbulent

---

[3] Jung, op. cit., par. 778-78.

and unstable, represents a transformation in individuation. The periods before and after these transitions tend to be relatively stable. The transitions show so much turmoil because the psyche is changing its basic orientation and perspective with regard to self and others.

Because many people have such an extended life span today, there is a significant transition period for them in late adulthood, into what is generally referred to as the years of "retirement." This does not necessarily mean cessation of all former work activities but rather signifies a transition from a more active life to a more reflective one. Earlier, adults carried major responsibilities in their various social and professional roles, and now they become more occupied with memories, reflections, and questions of spiritual meaning. This period of life is now coming under greater scrutiny by psychologists and psychotherapists in the expanding field of gerontology. What can still happen in old age from a psychological, developmental perspective is a topic of great interest. It is easy to see the decline: diminishing memory and learning capabilities, not to mention the athletic. We see the body starting to break down, and there are difficulties of all kinds physically. But this is not necessarily the case psychologically or spiritually. Further developments in individuation set in at this point that create another phase of life in late adulthood and extending into old age. Some of the greatest works of literature, art, music and philosophy have been created by people in this late stage of the individuation process.

The word "individual" means "undivided," and the phrase "individuation process" means "becoming undivided." As I will speak about psychological development, it will become clear why it is so important to become undivided, i.e., individuated, in the later stages of psychological development. In the course of life, the psyche gets divided into parts, i.e., conscious and unconscious. We necessarily separate from certain parts of the psyche at certain stages of development in order to gain a social identity, a persona. We leave parts of our self out of consciousness in order to adapt to social conditions and to find a place in our surrounding cultural contest. Then at a later stage of life, we have to go back and retrieve what has been left out or what has not been accessible so far. We have to bring ourselves along toward psychological wholeness, making the self as conscious as possible. Ultimately, the symbol of maximum achieved potential is the mandala, the circle. The circle contains all the parts; it is the whole. It can contain inner and outer conflicts without splitting and breaking. It can contain the maximum amount of information about oneself and the world, and hold it all together.

Each stage and each transition period in the individuation process have their specific challenges and requirements. I will outline the stages and the transition between briefly in the following pages.

Stage One: Childhood—The Era of the Mother

In the first stage, the individual takes form in the womb of the mother, then comes into the world at birth as a baby, and enters a period of infancy. This is the earliest part of the first stage of psychological development, and a lot can happen here that has an impact on later developments of personality. When you're in the mother's womb, you're in one world. Then when you're born, you come into another world, a transition from a dark to a light world. When the infant is born, it opens its eyes and ears, and begins to perceive things. It doesn't know where it is. It doesn't know who the people are, or even that they are people. It knows nothing at all about this world because its cognitive abilities are not yet developed. Imagine, you have no memory and no concepts! What is crucially important, though, is not understanding but forming an emotional attachment to this world. The newborn needs to become attached to somebody or something that will offer a warm reception and a motivation to want to stay in this world.

Many studies have been done over the last several decades by psychological researchers on the early relationship between mothers and infants. A theory called attachment theory has been developed to observe and speak about this phase. Attachment is like emotional glue that holds two people together so they want to be with each other. Another metaphor would be gravity— the smaller is held in place by the larger body. That gravity is love. As the mother and infant become attached and get to know each other by interacting, feeding, and playing, they become intimate and familiar. The infant wants to participate in life because it's a pleasure—it's a loving and nurturing world, and it's stimulating.

When this attachment is working well, the infant will begin to learn as its brain and body grow. It will begin to learn the customs, the language, the physical expression of emotion and feeling by observing and mirroring the one with whom it's most attached. This infancy stage, which lasts from the moment of birth until roughly the age of 18 months or 2 years, forms a transition from the other world and the world of the mother's womb to this world of persons, objects, and cultural values. If the transition is successful, the infant enters smoothly into the stage of childhood. If this attachment and transition from infancy into childhood does not take place well, the child may withdraw. Infants can actually decide, not cognitively but emotionally, to withdraw from participation in the world. Sometimes they refuse to take nourishment and don't survive. The main psychological task that needs to be achieved in this early stage is attachment. The mother figure doesn't have to be the biological mother. Whoever acts as the mother figure draws the child into life, makes the child want to stay and to participate in life. That's when attachment is achieved successfully.

This is the first part of the individuation process, and it takes place in the mother stage. This is sometimes called the paradise stage of individuation. It seems it should be paradise from the infant's point of view because everything basic and necessary for survival is provided— food, love, stimulation. The infant has nothing to do except to become attached and respond. Many people imagine early childhood as paradise. We all have some nostalgia for such a paradisal state. Mario Jacoby wrote a book called *Longing for Paradise*. That longing for paradise has been interpreted as a desire to return to this world of mother-infant nurturing, loving, playing. But that is a projection of an archetypal image. Mario Jacoby's book has a subtitle: *Psychological Perspectives on an Archetype*. He argues that the image of paradise is archetypal and therefore gets projected back into infancy from a later position, from the father stage of individuation, in the form of an imagined paradisal state. It is a projection backward of an archetypal image. Actually, infancy is not like that at all, either for child or parent. This early stage of life is much more tortured and complicated, as psychoanalytic authors have observed and written about. Nevertheless, the emphasis in this stage, which is dominated by the mother figure, is on holding and nurturing.

Paradise does not last forever, as we know from the Bible. As the child grows older, it begins to struggle with the attachment and wants more freedom. This is sometimes called "the terrible 2s." The child is looking for autonomy and beginning to develop a will of its own. If the baby is well attached, it wants to explore in ever wider circles. In this phase of childhood, the theme of separation begins to dominate the individuation process. As the child grows, it struggles to become more autonomous in life generally. Relationships with persons other than mother and father begin to take form. Breaking rules and breaking free, the child steps out of paradise and begins to encounter the world in a new way. The world opens up and expands, and the child wants to enter and participate in it. Here, you see a surge of ego development that instigates separation. The child wants to go its own way, to make its own choices, and to have what it wants whether this is approved by the mother or not. When it's hungry, it wants to eat. When it's tired, it wants to sleep. Here, you can see the first evidence of a drive to become an individual.

Moreover, as the ego develops, a division within the psyche between consciousness and the unconscious begins to open up. The child will show two personalities: a sweet conforming one and an obstreperous, disobedient one. It is the beginning of the persona-shadow development. What was one and simple becomes two and complex.

A child of this age still maintains a very strong attachment to the mother, although it is now a somewhat conflicted one. The presence of the father becomes increasingly important as another "pole" in the parental unit. He helps the child form a different relationship with the dominant mother, a position outside the former total dependency relationship. It's important that the father becomes involved with a child at an early age so the child is also equally attached to him. The father helps the child separate from the mother and makes a bridge to the outer world. He can bring the child with him into the outer world, the world of school and work, and the larger world of society and culture.

There's a problem if the father is not sufficiently present because of work or a divorce, or something else like illness has happened and the father is not available. Then, the mother has to also play the role of the father. The mother must take responsibility for not clinging to the child or trying to hold the child back from the outside world by trying to keep the child infant-like and close to her. She has to help the child let go of her. If the mother holds on too tightly, the child will have difficulty entering the next stage, which demands the development of a social persona, interaction with strangers, and eventually choosing a career and partner. So, it's very important that the mother allows and helps the child to separate.

When a mother brings such a child (4-6 years old) to play therapy or sand play therapy, the therapist needs to have an interview with the mother. This is necessary to discover whether the problem is that the mother is holding the child back too much or whether the father is absent. Then, the therapist can help the child through play to develop a sense of autonomy and independence. In that situation, the therapist represents the outside world, as the father would normally do, and introduces the child to a whole new round of possibilities. The sand play becomes a means of engaging with the outer world and separating from the mother.

Sometimes a child does not develop a secure attachment to the mother, and infancy is not paradise. If the mother is depressed and anxious, she will not be able to attach the baby to herself and therefore to life. This can result in an insecure child, even a suicidal child, a child who turns away from life. The therapist who receives a person who has had an insecure attachment to the mother can help this person through what is called a corrective experience in therapy. This is an experience that corrects and makes up for the earlier deficits. For cases like this, an essentially important aspect of the therapeutic process is the relationship to the therapist. The therapist must be very careful to nurture a stable and reliable presence for this type of client. If not, the insecurity will take over, and there will be a repetition of the earlier insecure attachment the person experienced with his or her mother.

The therapist countertransference attitude should move to the maternal position. The maternal countertransference attitude is receptive, nurturing, and patient, playing down any tendencies toward judgment or criticism. Perhaps the frequency of sessions will need to be increased. Once a week might not be enough— perhaps two or three times a week would be necessary. The therapy sessions should take place in an environment that feels safe and stable. The steady presence of the therapist, mirroring and making a deep emotional contact with the client is essential.

Stage Two: Young Adulthood—The Era of the Father

The child will eventually arrive at the important transitional stage of adolescence, normally beginning between ages 11 and 13. This is the beginning of the transition into adulthood. At this point, there is a need for a strong separation from the Mother World and into what I'll describe as the Father World. The adolescent shifts away from an attachment to the mother and other primary caregivers and goes over to attachment to peer groups and to other than parental adults. This can be a very confusing time emotionally. An old identity as a child is being outgrown and shed, like a snake shedding its skin as it grows, and a new identity as a young adult is now being formed around new identifications that gather around other than immediate family members.

The main psychological objective of this transition from childhood through adolescence and into early adulthood is adaptation—to the surrounding community of peers and adults and to the much larger cultural world in which all are embedded. The adolescent is a classic case of the liminal person—separated from the Mother World but not yet quite attached to the Father World. The adolescent is typically conflicted about this whole business of leaving childhood and the protective care of the Mother World: There is nostalgia for the old but also the realization that you can't go home again—there is no road back. And there is understandable resistance to entering the Father World where work and struggle, performance and judgment, and hierarchy of authorities dominate, a world so different from the guaranteed nurturance and protection in the Mother World.

In the Father World, people are graded on their performance. They're rewarded for hard work and achievement. And they're punished if they do not work hard, if they ignore the instructions of authorities, or if they withdraw from the tasks at hand. Reward and punishment, based on performance and work, belong to the Father World. As people pass through this stage of individuation, they make certain basic choices and decisions that indicate what kind of person they're going to be. These choices, whether made consciously or unconsciously, will give their life a particular shape and form. The decision to marry or not, to have children or not, the choice of what kind of career to pursue or what type of job to settle into, what type of education to pursue—all of these important life choices take place during this stage, and they will give that person a particular and distinct social identity, i.e., a persona.

Some people will resist making these decisions or make them half-heartedly, and often they find themselves stuck in the longing for the paradise of childhood. They don't want to "grow up." Peter Pan is the classic representative of this problem. They may start taking drugs because drugs are a way back to paradise. They will resist making a choice about a life partner. They will resist finding a suitable career or job and work at a very low level. This resistance to participating fully and actively in the Father World is based both on a negative father complex and on a pervasive longing to remain a child in paradise. When they look at what is required at school and the high demands of what is required in life in the adult world, it feels overwhelming to them. They feel weak, incapable, and afraid, so they withdraw into their room and play computer games or whatever, thinking: "I don't want to go to school— I don't want to leave home."

I had a client some years ago who came to me when he was in his late twenties. He had not finished school, and his parents were supporting him financially. He had just quit a job that he had managed to hold for a little while. He was very addicted to drugs, in particular to marijuana. He began smoking marijuana early in the morning and continued throughout the day. That robbed him of any motivation to move toward more independence in his life. The task I (gently) laid out for him to accomplish was first to stop smoking marijuana so that he could stay awake during the day. The second task was to go back and finish school. And the third task was to get more serious about a life partner. He already had a pretty steady girlfriend. I told him it would take a few years to fulfill these tasks completely but suggested we get started.

He was cooperative and understood the reason for this program, and he was open and intelligent, so the therapy worked. He needed direction and guidance, which his father had never provided because he was too busy in his own life and career to bother about this wayward son. After some years of steady progress along this path, he found himself no longer financially dependent on his parents. He has finished school, obtained a master's degree, gotten married, and had two children. On the surface, it looks as if he has achieved a lot in the way of individuation, but he's still a bit behind because of the years he lost in his addictions. He has achieved a measure of autonomy and independence from his family of origin, but he still tends to be dependent on others, notably now his wife. He hasn't quite reached the point of leaving the Mother World totally and fully entering the Father World of responsibility and maturity. But he has made a good start, and the work is still in process.

Archetypally speaking, it's the job of the father to help the child out of the Mother World and to enter the next stage of individuation. Both for girls and boys, it's necessary to have a kind of seduction into the world. It's like the first seduction in attaching the infant to a love object, a mother figure. But now the young person needs to become attached to something in the Father World that gives satisfaction and a feeling of belonging. Sometimes this has to go quite slowly and delicately with sensitive children. If it doesn't work, it's sometimes called "failure to launch," like a rocket sitting on the launch pad. It doesn't take off; it just sits there on the pad. This failure to launch can be a problem for psychotherapists who are often called into situations like this to try and help the child make the transition into the next stage of development. The other problem that can arise is if the mother doesn't want to let go of the child. Consciously or unconsciously, she wants to hold the child back and is retarding the child's progress. The mother has to let go and, in a sense, even push the child out of the nest.

Choices become very important during the Father stage because they can set the course for the rest of life. How free are we to make these choices? They will set the direction of life to come. There are many different pressures on a young person to make a certain specific kind of choice based on religion, gender, and social and academic possibilities. In some cultures, this choice has to be made quite early, and once it's made, it's difficult or impossible to change. In other cultures, there's more time to test various possibilities until something feels as if it fits the individual. Psychologists generally advocate spending more time in this phase and not to foreclose on possibilities too quickly, not to choose too early or too impulsively. There can also be family pressures. In some families, it's expected that the son will go into a certain type of career. If all the ancestors have been doctors, lawyers, architects, construction workers, fire-men or policemen, there is pressure to follow. The freedom of choice is sometimes not very great. The individual may have to struggle against pressures from the outside in order to make a good choice for himself or herself.

There is also the important issue of choosing what kind of life partner one is going to have. There is much more openness today to multiple possibilities, at least in Western cultures. The previous limitations were based on traditional role assignments. Today, young people have to struggle with these questions: What kind of love life do I want? What kind of sexual partner? What kind of life partner is best for me? Should it be male, female, or transgender? older or younger? This is an issue for many people nowadays in this stage of life. Again, psychologists would advise people not to force the choice too quickly. Let the choice emerge naturally, let it grow out of experience and personal feeling.

Stage Three: Mature Adulthood—The Age of the Individual

If you come to the point of saying, "I can't go on with my life like this anymore!" then what? If people choose to remain stuck in their habitual patterns, they often stagnate and become cynical about life. Life experience turns them bitter rather than wise. This part of individuation in the second half of life is about finding individual meaning. It becomes a circumambulation of the self, which happens in various ways. You begin to think for yourself in a new way and make choices based on an inner sense of what's right for you. These decisions may not conform to the expectations of the authorities, the higher-ups or superiors, so one has to be willing to make some sacrifices and changes. It is the twilight of the Father Stage.

This new pattern of being is what Erich Neumann wrote of as *centroversion*, which is a circumambulation around a center. How does one discover this center? It is what Jung identified as the self, the central organizing principle of the psyche. You can't get there just by ruminating and introspecting. Rumination and introspection can carry you a distance. If you just ask yourself, "What am I feeling? What do I like? What do I want?" it is a beginning, but it doesn't take you out of your ego-consciousness. Your ego is surrounded by a penumbra of consciousness, and you can expand outwardly into that consciousness, but you're locked into a limited mode of consciousness unless you start looking elsewhere. You need to open a closet or a door to the basement that you have not explored before. This is where dreams and active imagination become the key methods for moving beyond ego-consciousness and discovering the self.

Centroversion is a circumambulation but not around the ego. It's not: "What do I want? What do I like? What don't I like?" It's a circum-ambulation around the self. Now the ego is circling around something else, a different center. You are no longer the sun in the solar system; now you're the Earth, circling a greater body, the sun. Jungians have called this *relativization of the ego*—putting ego-consciousness into a secondary position within the psyche rather than a primary place. The ego is displaced by this and no longer holds absolute authority over decision-making. Jungians are famous for saying, "Let me consult the I Ching," or "Let me see what the dreams say." They want to consult with the self. In other words, you can't always give a spontaneous answer because you don't know what the self wants. You have to wait. And so, you don't make big decisions out of the ego anymore. Big decisions are made by taking into account a number of other factors. The unconscious has to have a say in the matter, and for this dreams and active imagination are the preferred sources of information.

A person who receives direction from an inner locus of control becomes more creative and can contribute something new and different to the world. This is not possible if one remains in the father stage, always imitating somebody or looking to an outside authority for instruction, direction or confirmation. In this later stage of individuation, one looks to the unconscious rather than to the outside world for inspiration and guidance. One looks for an inner teacher, an inner figure of authority rather than an outer one. Instead of asking what the father wants, what the teacher wants, what the boss wants, one begins asking what does the self want of me? How can I serve the self? How can I bring the spirit of the self into my life and into the world around me?

It's not an easy task to find one's inner direction or one's inner director. It takes some time and patience. The unconscious does not give simple instructions. Psychoanalysis can be helpful in making this major shift to inner-directedness. By looking at dreams, doing active imagination, and confronting parts of the self that might be very difficult to face, such as shadow aspects, one can gradually shift to an inner focus. This creates a separation from and transition out of the Father World of outer authority to the world of the individual, or what we call the self-directed world. This makes possible an adulthood that is more mature, inwardly directed and creative, offering leadership that is not possible in the earlier stage.

In each of these stages of the individuation process, one has a significantly different persona. In old age, if one lets go of one's positions and responsibilities in the world, the question becomes, "Who am I? What kind of persona can I have in this stage of life?" Some cultures have a tradition of the wise old man or the wise old woman, someone who is no longer active in life and yet embodies a precious quality that people look to for guidance. The Chinese sage Lao Tzu, for instance, is shown in pictures and paintings as a free and creative old personality—an old man whose smile symbolizes transcendence over the everyday concerns of life in the world.

Conclusion

In summary, the individuation process proceeds by two great movements: separation, and union, or synthesis, *separatio* and *coagulatio*, to use alchemical language. In the first movement, one separates psychologically from identification with mother and father, family of origin, then perhaps with the peer group, in order to develop an individual sense of self, of ego-consciousness and appropriate persona. On a deeper level, the ego gradually separates from the unconscious and from a type of fantasy life that is characteristic of childhood. One becomes more realistic, object-oriented and adapted to outer reality.

In the second half of life, one takes on board and includes in conscious identity some of the other figures and energies that have been left behind in the unconscious, and one's identity changes and becomes more complex. If you have been identified with the masculine side of the syzygy, you realize that you have an inner feminine, what Jung called the anima. Or if you have been identified with the feminine side, you discover that you have an inner masculine (animus). You aren't just masculine or feminine— you have several aspects. Synthesizing the opposites creates a new sense of self and a new identity made up of disparate parts of the self, conscious and unconscious.

This welding together of the conscious and unconscious makes for an individual that isn't based only on an ego identity but is on unconscious energies and sources. What had been divided becomes one, like a prime number, which cannot be divided by any other number. What you want to become as a fully realized, individuated personality is indivisible. Individuation—undivided. This reconciliation of the conscious and the unconscious in the second half of life is what Jung called, in his last book, "a mysterious conjunction" (*mysterium conjunctionis*). It is the union of the opposites.

Pillar Two
The Analytic Relationship

The second of the four pillars of Jungian psycho-analysis is the analytic relationship. How Jungian psychoanalysts understand and work in and with its complexity constitutes a central feature of their approach to clinical practice. This relation-ship is a sacred space, or temenos, in which analysis takes place.

When researchers have asked psycho-therapists of all the many schools that are in existence today what they regard as the single most important factor for a successful outcome in psychotherapeutic treatment, the answer is almost always the relationship between therapist and client. This is what makes the critical difference. It is the quality of relationship, not the therapist's theoretical persuasion, that is the most important factor. To that response, Jungian psychoanalysts would add: It's the relationship *plus* the cooperation of the unconscious and the self in the process that makes the critical difference between success and failure in analysis.

The relationship between analyst and client is the container that houses the therapeutic process and makes psychological change and development possible. The alchemical image of the *vas bene clausam* ("the well-sealed vessel") speaks of such a container. It is more than just an alembic made of glass. Rather, as the archetypal alchemist Maria Prophetissa said, "*Unum est vas*" ("the vessel is One"), meaning that "the whole secret lies in knowing about the Hermetic vessel."[1] If one understands this mystery, alchemical transformation of the base into the noble is possible. Without this, nothing transformational will happen. The alchemist had to procure the right vessel in order to do the job. In analysis, the relationship between analyst and client is the Hermetic vessel, and there is something mysterious and magical about it. It has power.

Relationships are critically important for psychological development from the moment of birth, all the way through life and until the very end. Many studies have shown that cognitive and emotional growth into psychological maturity is essentially dependent on good enough relationships. In the absence of such relationships,

---

[1] C.G. Jung, *Psychology and Alchemy*, par. 338.

development is either delayed, stunted, or goes entirely off the tracks into psychopathology. In analysis, this essential ingredient for growth is supplied by the therapeutic relationship. The complexity of this relationship has been the object of study by psychoanalysts since the earliest times and beginning in Freud's consulting room. Mario Jacobi, in his excellent small book *The Analytic Encounter*, writes about the complexities of the relationship and points out the analyst's position as being paradoxical: close to the client and distant at the same time. The closeness is a product of the intense interactive encounter between the two people in the room, and the distance is a result of the thinking the analyst is necessarily doing while processing the content clinically. The analyst must reserve a part of the mind to consider the case material from a theoretical and clinical perspective. This position has also been described as "one foot in and one foot outside" the encounter that's taking place in the therapeutic session. This can be an awkward position at times, but it is necessary to maintain for the sake of the client. The analyst is both in the alchemical process and tending it from the outside at the same time. This is a professional responsibility.

When people decide to look for a psychotherapist, they generally have a pretty strong feeling that they need somebody to help with an immediate and pressing psychological issue. They can't go it alone anymore. At that point, absent an acute crisis, it's a good idea to visit a few psychotherapists if possible. Go into their office, have a session and ask yourself afterward: "What was the feeling like there between the two of us? Is this a good fit?" The fit does not have to be perfect, but it has to be good enough. There has to be a "click," a connection, and a gut feeling of trust and confidence that the therapist can understand you. Most likely this first impression will be based on a projection that resonates with a past relationship—with mother, father, grand-parent, uncle, etc.

In the initial session, Jungian analysts will often suggest meeting a few times before deciding whether to enter into a long-term analytic commitment. If at that point the answer is "yes," the sessions can go on without a specific ending point in the future. If not, and it is agreed that this is not a good fit, the therapy relationship can stop there. If there is a difference of opinion, it can be discussed, and this may lead to an important insight and further sessions.

In the first several sessions, Jungian psycho-analysts will also ask themselves: "Is this somebody I can work with?" Analysis is very individual and personal, and analysts have their limitations. They need to know what these are. Perhaps the analyst can't understand or empathize with the client's presenting problem, or can't imagine a way into the client's mental framework or psychological makeup because they are too different. Or the client may present a problem that touches the analyst's personal complexes too deeply and painfully. In that case, the analyst would be wise to refer the person to somebody who might be a better choice.

One rightfully expects that analysts will know quite a bit about therapeutic and analytic relationships from their training, study, and experience. They are prepared to understand that this relationship can become emotionally charged and psychologically complex. In the profession, this complexity is referred to as transference/countertransference. This two-part term has to do with the psychological levels that develop within the analytic relationship. The reference is to conscious and unconscious dynamics that generate strong emotional currents in the interactive field. The diagram below indicates the complexities in the relationship.

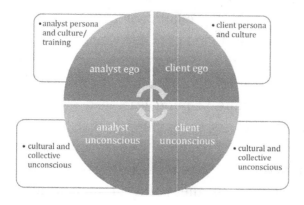

Freud and the Origin of "Transference"

The term "transference" was first used by Freud to speak about the psychological attitude his patients developed toward him in his role as their psychoanalyst. The German word he used, *Übertragung*, derives from the verb that means literally "to carry over, to transfer" something from one place or time to another. Freud interpreted the strong emotional reactions of his patients as a transfer of feelings from childhood, when the child looked upon the parent as magically powerful, for better or worse, and out of this a type of infantile dependency developed. Freud saw that this childish attachment to himself took hold more and more powerfully as patients regressed in analysis to earlier stages of psychological development, even to the infantile stage of total dependency on the caregiver. In this state, the analyst became an object of fear and desire for the client, and the client felt utterly vulnerable to the analyst's will. This gave the doctor immense emotional power. The transference was a kind of magic wand that enabled the analyst to cure or to crush the client's fragile psyche that lay quivering in his hands.

This state of mind was seen by the early psychoanalysts as similar to what happens to patients under hypnosis. The hypnotist assumes a remarkable degree of suggestive power over the hypnotized to the point of almost magical proportions. Freud had studied hypnosis and observed its powerful effects in the Paris clinic of Janet, and he began to use hypnosis in the treatment of hysteria. Under hypnosis, the patient would receive his suggestions for changes in their habits of thinking and behaving, and these would have a beneficial effect for at least a brief period of time.

The use of hypnosis as a method of medical and psychological treatment had been developed in the late 18th and 19th centuries beginning with Franz Anton Mesmer and his theory of "animal magnetism."[2] James Braid applied it to reduce certain physiological functions, Hyppolyte Bernheim then took a psychological turn with it and spoke of "suggestibility" achieved under hypnosis, and Jean-Martin Charcot and Pierre Janet introduced it into psychiatry. Freud studied briefly with Janet in Paris, and both thought of hypnotism as a procedure for contacting the unconscious and making use of its extraordinary powers. Under hypnosis, patients would reveal memories and thoughts that were not accessible during the normal waking state. Hypnotic suggestion also seemed to be quite successful in treating certain mental illnesses. For example, if someone had a trauma and was suffering from

---

[2] For a complete discussion, see *The Discovery of the Unconscious* by H. Ellenberger.

flashbacks, a command could be given under hypnosis: "Do not think about that trauma ever again. Just put it into a black box, close the box, and bury it." This would cancel the flashbacks, and the patient would be relieved. It was like magic. Symptoms could simply be dismissed, and they seemed to disappear.

However, Freud later discovered that the cure did not last very long so he abandoned the use of hypnosis in psychoanalysis. Instead, he had his patients simply talk freely while lying on a couch with him sitting quietly behind them and out of sight. When they did this, he discovered that they entered a quasi-hypnotic state and developed a powerful fantasy relationship to him. The young women he was treating in Vienna in the 1890s regressed to a state of childhood, and in that state they would think and feel about the invisible analyst who was sitting silently behind them as a powerful father figure. This is what Freud called "the transference," a carry-over of feelings from the past and placed into the present situation. Thus, the present becomes the past and the past becomes the present. Temporality collapses. The state of mind induced in the transference was similar to a hypnotic trance but not as dissociated from normal ego-consciousness because the patient was fully awake.

When Freud was working in the early days of psychoanalytic treatment with his colleague Josef

Breuer and both were seeing patients using the same method, they simultaneously discovered that their patients also developed very strong erotic feelings toward them. This immediately suggested father-daughter incest. Freud took this at first to be evidence of an actual incestuous relationship in the client's childhood. Later, he changed his mind and thought of it as a sexual fantasy and wish from childhood rather than a concrete event. The transference was a repetition of the erotic wish the girl earlier had had toward her father. From this, Freud concluded that children do have sexual fantasies and desires. Even though they do not normally engage in explicitly sexual acts, they have sexual wishes and fantasies, and it is these that are later carried over into the relationship with the analyst. This sexual feeling was so strong in one of his young women patients that Josef Breuer, who found himself responding to it strongly in his countertransference, decided to abandon his career as a psychoanalyst because it threatened his marriage.

In the psychoanalytic setting, the simple instruction is to say whatever comes to mind, don't resist or block it, just bring it out and say it. Freud's patients must have felt great relief to be able to speak their feelings openly to the father figure sitting behind them. One of Josef Breuer's patients, Anna O, named psychoanalytic treatment "a talking cure." She felt healed after talking about her hidden and repressed feelings.

Jung and Transference

Jung read Freud's works during his early years of training as a psychiatrist at the University of Zurich's Burgholzli Klinik, and in 1907, he went to visit him in Vienna. They spent several days in long and intense discussions. Jung was a young and up-and-coming psychiatrist at the time, 32 years old, and upon meeting Freud, he admired him and his genius. By the time they met, he had already started to use Freud's method of psychoanalysis with a few of his patients in the Burgholzli Klinik. Jung's first psychoanalytic patient was Sabina Spielrein, a young Russian Jewish woman, 18 years old, who was brought to the Burghölzli Klinic for treatment of what Jung diagnosed as "psychotic hysteria." Jung thought she was a suitable subject for psychoanalysis, and as he started using Freud's method, he soon discovered the awesome power of transference. Spielrein had exactly the type of reaction toward him that Freud had described in his books.

When Jung met Freud for the first time, at one point in the conversation, Freud asked him, "And what do you think about the transference?" Jung's immediate reply was, "Transference is all!" Freud said, "Ah, you have understood." Freud was pleased to get that answer from Jung. On the subject of transference as the key to treatment and cure, it seemed, they saw eye to eye. As a result of these discussions in Freud's practice room in Vienna, they formed a close professional, collegial relationship. In that relationship, Jung also discovered that he had deep and irrational-based feelings toward Freud. This, too, was a type of transference, but man-to-man. At one point, Jung confessed in a letter to Freud that he had a kind of "religious crush" on him that had homosexual overtones, which scared him because of a childhood incident of sexual abuse by an admired older man.

Freud was not exactly Jung's analyst. He didn't lie on Freud's couch and have a formal analysis, but he did send Freud some of his dreams and received interpretations by mail. An intimate and highly charged emotional relationship quickly developed in which Jung was given the position of a favored son and heir, and Freud received the position of an idealized older father-teacher-mentor. This was quite understandable since Freud was about 20 years older than Jung and a strong paternal figure in his own family and circle of followers. Jung's was the kind of love a young man feels when he becomes enamored of an admired teacher. But as Jung soon realized, there was even more to it than that. For him, Freud was a numinous figure, almost godlike, therefore the term "religious crush." Later in his life, Jung would speak of this type of projection as an "archetypal transference." This is a projection of an archetypal image that far exceeds a person's personal experience of a parent. In fact, Jung's father was not a strong figure in his eyes. Much larger loomed his grandfathers, Samuel Preiswerk and C.G. Jung, the illustrious father of Paul Jung whose parentage was traced in the family to Wolfgang Goethe. In Basel where Jung grew up, too, there were famous men like Bachofen, Burkhardt and Nietzsche who had impressed him as a youth and occupied an elevated position in his psyche. He knew a genius when he met one, and in Freud, he found just that.

For many reasons, the transference relationship in which powerful emotional reactions develop—whether love or admiration, hate or rivalry—became a distinct focus of study in an evolving field of psychoanalysis. In a letter to Freud, Jung wrote of psychoanalysis as "a most dangerous method" because of the emotions it unleashes. At first, it was thought that all of this emotion came from the side of the patient, as a repetition of childhood wishes and fantasies. Later, the founders realized that transference does not remain so one-sided but also has a powerful effect on the analyst. Hence the term counter-transference: the analyst's emotions are a reaction, a "counter" response, to the patient's transference. They began to look more carefully at the analyst's side of the therapeutic couple. It was not only that the patient was caught up in this powerful emotional field, but the doctor was affected by it as well. Two people are in this relationship, and they share a common atmosphere and emotional space. It's like a bath in which both are immersed. They are both in the water, and this is the medium in which the analysis is conducted. The nature of the emotional atmosphere between them affects all the transactions that take place in this space. When the transference develops in this relationship, so does the countertransference, and the emotional atmosphere becomes intensely charged.

Jung was an extremely sensitive and intuitive man, so he could easily pick up on feelings in the atmosphere. When a transference developed, he was aware that irrational emotions were becoming increasingly prominent in the relationship. But he also noticed that it wasn't just the patient's emotions that were being stirred up. His own feelings were also responding. So, Jung began speaking about the analyst's contribution to this atmosphere. Emotion isn't just coming from the patient, it's also coming from the analyst. With his first psychoanalytic patient, Sabina Spielberg, Jung felt that he was being drawn into a strong emotional attachment as a kind of erotic friendship developed. He discussed this patient in his correspondence with Freud and confessed that he had learned something important about his hitherto unrecognized "polygamous components despite all self-analysis."[3] In their discussions, Freud gave it the name countertransference and admitted that he had also had such experiences in his psychoanalytic practice.[4]

Jung's experience with Spielrein was so intense that he felt it was dangerous for him as a professional medical man and a husband. It had enticed him into a relationship that could spin out of control. Because of this danger, it became generally recommended that part of psychoanalysts' training should include undertaking analysis themselves. It is essential for psychoanalysts to understand and themselves to experience what can happen in this type of professional relationship. Both Jung and Freud were aware that countertransference has its roots in the analyst's unconscious. It's not a superficial, transient response; it comes out of a deep part of the psyche and has great value if properly used. Analysts need to understand where this response is coming from within themselves, to put some safeguards on this most dangerous method of psychological treatment, and also to learn to use it for the benefit of the patient.

---

[3] W. McGuire (ed.), *The Jung-Freud Letters*, p.207.
[4] Ibid., p. 231.

This type of relational complexity between doctor and patient in psychoanalysis was completely unlike other medical specialties where the doctor treats the patient from an Apollonic distance and refrains from getting involved emotionally as much as possible. In the specialty of psychiatry, too, as it was practiced in the context of hospital medical treatment, doctors kept a clinically detached perspective in their work with the mentally ill. Psychoanalysts, on the other hand, became specialists on the topic of relationships and how they assist or hinder mental health. The acknowledgment that the analytic relationship is rooted in projections from the patient to the analyst and from the analyst to the patient opened the field to much wider and deeper understanding. It was now possible to think about the variety of contents from the unconscious that could be projected onto the relationship.

This expansion of what is possible in a psychotherapeutic relationship, however, was not well received by Freud because it opened the door to features that were not incestuous or sexual and therefore did not conform to his Oedipal theories. He had a rather narrow focus on one particular type of projection, while Jung suggested that one can project whatever is unconscious and goes for the "hook" put out by the other.

In more recent times, some Jungian psycho-analysts have spoken about mutual transference rather than using the term countertransference. The view holds that both analyst and patient are projecting freely onto each other. The term countertransference assumed that the analyst was responding to the patient's transference, which held priority. But what if projection simply occurs from the analyst's side because of what the patient looks like, or the way the patient acts or behaves? What if it's not in response to trans-ference, but simply comes out of the analyst's unconscious in response to a "hook" that the patient offers and is most likely unaware of? The analyst would be trained to observe this carefully and could presumably become conscious of the projection quickly and be able to contain it and not allow it to contaminate the interactions with the patient. Maybe in the first session or even in the initial phone call, feelings arise toward a prospective patient. It's essential to observe these initial reactions that appear before there is an experience of the transference that might be coming from the patient.

Around 25 years after these initial dis-coveries and discussions with Freud, Jung was invited to give a series of lectures at the Tavistock Clinic in London. He began by talking about a patient's dreams, but the audience pressed him to speak about transference as well so he adjusted his program and gave them a lively and interesting lecture from a few notes he had scribbled onto an envelope in his hotel room the night before. He started out by saying that he's always happy when there is no transference. This was a provocative comment to the audience of mostly Freudian psychoanalysts whose bread-and-butter topic was transference. But Jung had discovered during the course of his work with many patients that transference and counter-transference could make it difficult and get in the way, or become an obstacle, to a deep analysis of the unconscious. He preferred to work with dreams and active imagination in sessions that were relatively free of transference. But is this really possible? He knew well enough that it is not, and he did go on to deliver a substantial lecture on the subject of transference.

At first, the idea was that one person, the patient, was bringing all the emotional intensity and transference into the sessions. Later, it was recognized there were two people involved in the dynamics and that transference projections were contributed by both. In his essay "On the Psychology of the Transference," Jung presented a diagram of the interactive field. The diagram below shows the complexity of the field as it exists between analyst A and client P, where A' and P' indicate the unconscious of each:

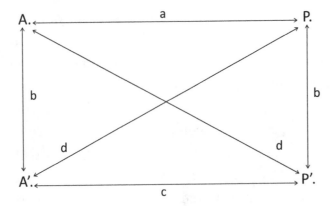

The arrows indicate the vectors of the relational field as follows:

(a) the vertex of conscious dialogue between analyst and patient;

(b) the vertex of internal dynamics within analyst and patient;

(c) the vertex of unconscious interaction between analyst and patient;

(d) the vertex of mutual transference/countertransference projections.

The field of psychoanalysis thus moved on to a view of an exchange between two people in a relational space that is highly interactive.

The most intriguing part of the relationship is level "c." At level "c," there is a meeting of the two psyches that is going to be critically transformational for both analyst and client. It's a type of fusional relationship where the two psyches meet and become one. They form a new, mutually available sense of the self. The relationship at level "c" is powerful and enduring. It has what

Jung said produces *kinship libido*, the feeling of being deeply related in a quasi-biological fashion. It makes for an enduring bond between analyst and client who are engaged in a mutual enterprise of transformation.

In an essay titled "Problems of Modern Psychotherapy," Jung wrote about four stages of analysis. The first stage is confession. In this stage, the analyst is in a position of simply receiving and accepting the confession, secrets, or shadow material that the client brings. In the second stage, elucidation, the analyst is more active. He or she offers explanations for the client's feelings, such as conflicts between the conscious and the unconscious, or conflicts between the client and his or her surrounding world. This is a stage of psychological explanations. The third stage is called education. The analyst offers clients help to better understand themselves and their relationship to the outer world. Jung spends most of the essay discussing the fourth stage, which is transformation. This is the stage in which the transference and countertransference relationship takes on vital importance. The analyst enters into the relationship more deeply than in the first three stages. Both the analyst and the client are part of the transformation that takes place in the fourth stage. This is what Jung writes about most deeply in "On the Psychology of the Transference," where he details the process of this merger of psyches.

Jung would argue that dialogue is preferable to one-sided interpretation if change is to be brought about. However, it can be a considerable length of time to arrive at a place where mutual dialogue is possible. If the transference and countertransference dynamics are strong, it can take a long time to resolve them enough for an open exchange, which the term "dialogue" implies, to become possible. It requires a shift from transference/countertransference dynamics to mutuality of communication. It is a signal of developing maturity in the relationship when this becomes possible. This type of exchange is what Jung was saying he prefers when he announced so boldly that he was glad when there was no transference.

Some Practical Considerations

Transference can be intractable, however, and the psyche is capable of extraordinary distortions and will often overcome reality-testing in favor of projection. The projection of a mother-image onto a male analyst is frequent. The same is true of age. When I was a young analyst, I would sometimes receive projections of being a wise old man. What the unconscious is seeking and needs will be projected onto the analyst. If the unconscious is seeking a mother, whether loving or negative, that is what will be projected on to the analyst, never mind gender or age. If the unconscious is seeking a wise old man, it will be projected even if the age of the analyst is not correct. When a strong transference is active, the analyst has to make a decision whether to try to reduce its intensity or even remove it through interpretation, or to *carry the transference* for the time being because it's what the patient needs. Some analysts prefer to aggressively interpret the transference, feeling that it might bring consciousness into the relationship and move it along toward the possibility of dialogue. Others prefer to carry the transference out of respect for what the unconscious needs at this particular juncture in that person's life.

If an analyst brings his or her own complex into the therapeutic setting and it enters the relationship, it is recommended that the analyst take that case to supervision. Analysts need to work on what they are bringing into the session so they are not distorting the process with their own neurotic or unconscious needs and projections. Analysts are also trained to use their countertransference reactions to become more empathic toward a patient, to understand a patient better. Psychic communication, both conscious and unconscious, is critically important for the analytic work. If there is little transference or countertransference projection in the relationship, however, the analysis stays on a basically rational level.

It's of vital importance to keep in mind that unconscious contents projected in the counter-transference could bring trauma to the client. At the beginning of this chapter, I discussed the need for a suitable fit between analyst and client. Sometimes it happens that the analyst does not offer a suitable fit and, in fact, is not good for the client. Perhaps an analyst's past problems are triggered by a particular client. This is certainly not useful or therapeutic. If this is the case, a decision needs to be made whether it's best for the analysis to be terminated. Sometimes the client has to decide, "This therapy is not helpful to me—it's actually harmful." If that's the experience, and the client has to trust his or her experience, he or she would have to stop working with that particular analyst. The question is: When is it bad enough to stop the analysis? Sometimes there are very difficult periods when the relationship is quite conflicted, but that might be a necessary stage in the process. So how do you judge? When is it bad enough? I think it's when one leaves the session feeling it has been really hurtful or toxic, and especially if this happens a few times in succession.

Sometimes the question arises: How long should therapy last? When is it time to stop?[5] There are different ways to decide when to end an analytic relationship. The rule of thumb that most Jungian analysts use is, as one of my teachers, Joseph Wheelwright, once said: "I always let the client fire me. I don't fire the client." If a client feels benefit from the sessions, feels that he or she is becoming more conscious, developing psychologically or spiritually, and wants to continue—and if the analyst is in good health, not ready to retire or move away—then the relationship can proceed indefinitely. I think the longest I have worked with a client is about 30 years. A typical Jungian analysis will last between two to five years. In that period of time, there will be many changes in the quality and intensity of the relationship. It might begin with a lot of transference, which then dies away and transforms into a dialogue. New energy enters, perhaps a new project or a new feeling, and over time the relationship develops and matures. It does not remain static.

A student once told me that at the end of three years of analysis there was uncertainty between both herself and her analyst whether or not to conclude it. She had this dream the night

---

[5] For a full discussion of this, see H. Abramovitch, "When Is It Time to Stop? When Good Enough becomes Bad Enough."

before a session: "Entering the analytic space, everything was as usual, except my chair had been removed and in its place was a backpack lying on the floor, fully packed for a journey. I looked at the analyst, who was standing. He indicated for me to sit in his chair, the only one in the room." End of dream. This made it clear to both of them that the client was now ready to be her own analyst and continue the process of integration on the "the journey of life." Sometimes dreams give very clear indications. When the analytic relationship is about to be concluded, the analyst will want to have some confidence that the person can continue the individuation process on his or her own. By observing dreams, doing active imagination, having meaningful and deep relationships with friends or partners—in this way, individuation continues.

Types of Transference

Transference is a type of projection. There are many different categories of projection, of which I will discuss three. Each of them can play a role in the transference situation. The most archaic and psychologically hidden and unexamined type of projection is what Jung called "participation mystique." This is an unconscious identity between subject and object. It is a projection to somebody with whom one becomes identified in a twin-like merger of two psyches. In consciousness, there is no difference between the two personalities. When this happens in the transference, the client feels that the analyst is just like they are—twins, exactly the same. In this kind of transference, the client would become upset if the analyst said or did something that was different from what they were thinking or feeling. When this difference appears, it's quite shocking to the client. This is the so-called twinship transference.

The second type of transference is what Jung spoke about as the projection of archetypal images onto the analyst. When something archetypal is projected onto another person, he or she becomes larger than life, not quite human, as celebrities and famous people are often looked upon. They are more like cartoon figures, or idealized gods and goddesses. When this kind of transference takes place in analysis, the client might feel that the therapist knows everything and is immensely powerful. The therapist has the capacity to heal or to make sick and has extraordinary qualities that are almost beyond imagining. The analyst may appear to the patient like a Great Father or a Great Mother figure, a god or goddess, boundless and without personal needs or troubles, self-sufficient and immortal— at the minimum, somebody very different from ordinary human beings. This can introduce an element of fear into the relationship because the analyst is so powerful that he or she can help you, heal you, or really wound and hurt you. An element of fear creeps in when the projection is so archetypal and numinous. This is called an "idealizing transference."

The third type of projection originates in a more superficial layer of the unconscious, the personal unconscious. This would be a projection of a complex or figures from one's own personal history. When this type of projection occurs, the feelings of the patient toward the therapist tend to be very mixed and conflicted. Most complexes, when projected, involve an early experience of trauma. One's personal experience from childhood, perhaps with one's mother or father, enters the transference. The client begins to feel toward the analyst the way they did as a child toward a parent. The feelings about the therapist in this case depend on the experience with parents, whether positive or negative, particularly in early childhood. This type of projection can easily turn into a so-called negative transference. It produces feelings of suspicion or mistrust, of needing to be very careful or the therapist might explode and get angry. Or it might be that the client had loving feelings toward parents as a child that were for some reason not accepted. That would make the client want to come close to the therapist, maybe even move into the therapist's home and live with the therapist the way a child does with the original family.

We can speak of positive transference and negative transference. Positive transference can be very idealizing, loving, and admiring, and negative transference can be angry, afraid, and suspicious. There is also what we call "mirror transference," which is the feeling of wanting to be mothered, held, and nurtured by the therapist. And there is what we call the "erotic transference," which is fusional. It's a transference that wants to become united with the object of desire sexually, to bond in a loving relationship with the analyst.

Types of Countertransference

As there are several types of transference, so there are types of countertransference. To begin, there is a distinction to be made between stable attitudes and momentary reactions in countertransference. A countertransference attitude is a basic position that a therapist assumes in relation to every case. It's part of the analyst's professional stance for receiving clients who come for therapy. Analysts will typically develop a stable countertransference attitude as they practice over a period of time and form habits. An attitude is a habit, a consistent way of receiving the client.

One may think of at least four basic types of countertransference attitude. The first is the "maternal countertransference attitude." This is the view that assumes the clients are coming to be contained, held, and nurtured. The assumption is that patients are coming to therapy for empathy and understanding. With this attitude, the therapist meets the clients from the position of a mother, a maternal approach. If you are with a therapist who has a maternal countertransference, you tell them what happened to you recently, and they will empathize with you and assure you that they understand that it must be very painful and hurtful. The therapist can be a man or woman—it doesn't matter.

Then there is a contrasting approach that is based on the father archetype, the "paternal countertransference attitude." This is an attitude that receives the patient with a plan and with ideas for how to move forward in life to better functioning and adaptation. It's directive and based on the assertion of authority and power in the sessions. A therapist with this attitude assumes that what clients basically need is help in changing their life and becoming more successful in their daily activities. It's the assumption that clients arrive in therapy for direction or a plan. If your therapist has a paternal attitude, he or she might listen to your story and ask, "If you had that to do over again, how would you do it differently?" The analyst could give you some advice, show you where you made your mistake, and try to teach you how not to make that same mistake again. Analysts with a paternal countertransference attitude may present themselves as role models or teachers.

Thirdly, there is the "hermetic counter-transference attitude," which references the Greek god Hermes. Hermes is a youthful god and specializes in transformation and creative play-fulness. The analyst with a hermetic attitude assumes that what the patient is coming for is transformation, a process of change, to learn to be more creative and playful in life. Here, the emphasis is not on empathy with feelings or giving advice or direction, but on playing with the patient and creating an atmosphere of freedom to dream. Hermetic analysts are like magicians or tricksters, and they do unexpected things. Hermetic analysts might say something in a session that seems totally irrelevant, something that just occurred to them or entered their imagination. If you are the client, you are just stopped in your tracks. You are made to think out of the box of your habitual ruminations. The hermetic analyst may say something that makes you laugh. What the analyst wants is to bring psychic movement. Hermes is a god of wind. Hermetic analysts are pleasantly unpredictable. You don't know what they're going to say or do next.

Jung was sometimes a hermetic psycho-therapist. Once in a while, he would stage a strong emotional reaction in order to get a rise, to get something moving, to break a habit or an old and dead form of talking or thinking. One time a patient brought him a dream about a golden scarab beetle that was doing something extraordinary. Jung was fascinated by this image, and while he was listening to the dream, he heard a noise behind him. His house was on the lake, with a garden around the house, and there was something tapping outside on the window. Jung suddenly and dramatically jumped up from his chair, threw open the window, and grabbed an insect in his hand. It was a garden beetle similar to the scarab beetle of the dream. He held it in his hand and proclaimed dramatically, "Here is your beetle!" It was utterly shocking to this conservative young woman that Jung would do something unexpected like this. Jung called this coincidence a synchronicity and reported that this was a turning point in the therapy. The unexpected hermetic gesture produced a transformation in the patient's attitude. It broke the mold of a habitual way of thinking and opened the way into a field of new exploration.

The fourth attitude I will mention here is the "maieutic countertransference attitude." The word "maieutic" goes back to the Greek and is a reference to the nurse who assisted women in giving birth. She is present at the birth of a new life, a child. The analyst with a maieutic attitude will receive clients with the assumption that clients want a new beginning. They want to give birth to a new future, a new possibility, and the analyst (male or female) will help them in that process. The maieutic psychotherapist's attitude is that of a midwife. This is a woman who comes to your house when you're about to give birth and assists in the labor and delivery of the baby. This type of countertransference attitude is not very interested in the past. It's interested in creating a new future and giving birth to fresh, innovative attitudes, directions, and ideas—basically, delivering new energy into the client's outworn life.

The maieutic analyst often spends a lot of time on dreams, because dreams are the womb of the future—they contain the seeds of possibility. This type might also be interested in astrology charts, because astrology can offer symbols for thinking about the future, near or distant. This maieutic analyst is not so interested in following the case for a long time. A midwife is just there to deliver the baby and hand it over to the mother. When the job is done, she has finished. This tends to be an intuitive type of analyst who can look deeply into the unconscious and the future. They might act as a kind of medium or fortune-teller. But they are easily bored by the basic tasks of raising children and taking care of them. The value is in the birthing of the new.

I remember a story a French woman told me some years ago. She had a session with Jung when she was a young woman around 18 years old. A friend who knew Jung quite well brought her to see him. He said to Jung, "I'd like you to do a session with this young lady to see if you can give her some guidance, because she doesn't know what to do with her life." The woman told me that she was with Jung for just an hour, and he asked her some questions about her life. After he listened to her intently for 30 or 40 minutes, he gave her the answer. He saw her future, and he helped give birth to it. He said: "On the basis of what you've told me, I can see that you are meant to be a doctor and to become a psychiatrist. Yes, this is what you are meant to do." She told me that session with Jung changed her life and gave her life direction. And that is exactly what she did. I met her when she was 50 years old and she was a psychiatrist. That was a maieutic session. I don't think Jung followed up on her for very long. Maybe he heard occasionally from her, but basically, it was just one session. He gave birth to a new idea and direction, which she then had to take care of herself, like raising a child. After 20 years, she had matured and become the person Jung had seen in her psyche, in her potential.

A skillful therapist can move through all four of these different attitudes, depending on what the client needs at a particular time. It's important for therapists to become conscious of their basic countertransference attitude and to reflect on it. After establishing the basic mode, the therapist can and should become more flexible and try other positions.

Pillar Three

Dreams as a Way to Wholeness

Jungian psychoanalysts place great value on working with the dreams of their clients (also with their own dreams). Dreams can tell both the analyst and client what is going on below the surface of consciousness. The unconscious is another realm with a life of its own, and often it runs quite contrary to what is going on in the world of consciousness. When a person is sleeping, another type of thinking is taking place that is different from waking thought. Dreams can give us important information about what is going on within ourselves and about possible developments for the future. But beyond that, and more important for the outcome of analysis, is that dreams build the way to psychological wholeness.

The first book by Freud that Jung read and digested when he was a student in psychiatry at the Berghölzli Clinic in Zurich was *The Interpretation of Dreams*. It's generally considered to be Freud's greatest work and has become a classic. Jung was immediately fascinated by Freud's keen insights into the dreaming mind and what it can reveal about a person's hidden motives and repressed feelings. Dreams became a major consideration in his work with patients and in his reflections about his own life. Working with dreams has become a central feature of Jungian psychoanalysis ever since.

If you ask people you meet socially, for instance striking up conversations in restaurants or at parties, if dreams are interesting or important to them, most will say they don't remember their dreams. Or they might say they don't have dreams. You can tell them that scientific research has shown that everybody dreams during their sleep; in fact all mammals dream. Whether you remember them or not is another question, but you do have dreams. Then the person you're talking to might say, "So what? Maybe I do dream, but why should I pay any attention to them? What does it matter?" You can answer, "Well, if you don't pay attention to your dreams, you're missing out on an important part of what your mind is doing. It's thinking while you're sleeping, so aren't you curious to know what you're thinking about while you're sleeping?" They might become curious and start taking note of their dreams. And so it begins.

When you meet these same people a few weeks later, they might tell you, "I've had some dreams and recorded them, but I don't understand anything they're saying. Are they trying to tell me something?" "Yes," you can reply and smile enigmatically. They will most likely insist that their dreams are absolute nonsense, so of course, they can't make heads or tails of them. Then you can answer, "Well, your dreams are speaking another language, a symbolic language. You have to learn that language if you want to understand what they're saying to you, or about you." This is the beginning of reflecting on dreams. What do they tell us? To understand them is not particularly easy, but it's what the Jungian analyst is trained to do. This is called "dream interpretation," and it's what Freud wrote his famous book about.

The dream has a message, but it needs to be interpreted in order to be understood. That's why Pharaoh asked Joseph to explain to him what his dreams were telling him. Joseph was a genius and saved the land from starvation with his interpretation of Pharaoh's dreams. The Jungian psychoanalyst is a kind of modern version of Joseph. People come with dreams that need interpretation in order to become meaningful. They might be messages that will save the dreamer's life, or at least improve its quality by offering the opportunity to become more conscious of self and others.

In this chapter, I will discuss how Jungian psychoanalysts work with dreams in their practices. To begin, let's engage in a bit of fantasy—you are going to visit Jung for a consultation. Imagine that you have received Jung's name from a friend or a former patient of his, and to your great surprise, he has accepted your request for a consultation. Perhaps you have some psychological conflicts or are suffering from a psychological malady like depression, and you

would like to have some sessions of analysis with the famous Professor Jung.

When the day arrives and it's time for your first session, you approach his house at the end of an allee of tall trees. You confront this impressive entrance.

Above the door is a carved stone with a saying from the Delphic oracle: VOCATUS ATQUE NON VOCATUS DEUS ADERIT.

When you stop for a moment and read this, you ask yourself, am I entering a temple? What does this saying mean, and why is it above his doorway? You pull the old ringer on the side of the door and a servant opens the door. You are admitted into Jung's house. The servant guides you up a staircase to the library on the first floor.

As you enter, Jung welcomes you and leads you into his small private consulting room behind the library. He invites you to sit down on a chair across from him and indirectly facing him. When you are comfortably seated, he looks at you intently and asks: "Well, why have you come to see me? What can I do for you? Are you having a problem?" Jung has very penetrating eyes, and you feel he is looking directly into your soul.

71

When he asks you that question, you think you'd better be straight with him. You'd better be honest and tell him your real problem, and why you need his help.

You begin by explaining your present situation: where you are in life; where you are stuck and having difficulties; what you are suffering from; your history of trauma and wounding. In short, you tell him your life story. Jung listens intently and does not say anything. You finish by asking: "Professor Jung, can you help me? Can you give me advice? What should I do?" Jung looks at you and quietly says: "I have no idea what you should do, no idea whatsoever how you should live your life. I can't give you answers to such important questions. But if you bring me your dreams, we can look at them together and see if your psyche has the answer. If there is guidance, that's where it will be."

That would be your first session and the beginning of your analysis with Professor Jung. The question is: What do your dreams say? Maybe you've never thought about your dreams before. Maybe you never thought they were of any interest or value. But here is the famous professor Jung saying the solutions come from your dreams; not from him, but from your unconscious. So he suggests that together you take a look, go into your inner world, and see what your dreams are saying. The dreams will be worked with and interpreted as a means to psychotherapy.

Jung's approach to dreams of his patients was not to study them scientifically. Rather, working with dreams was a practical exercise in healing the soul. Jung had a vast amount of practice working with dreams, analyzing, and interpreting them. He gave it a great deal of thought, and he wrote extensively on the subject. Jungian psychoanalysts after him have basically followed his guidelines and procedures. This is what we will delve into now, beginning with the structure of dreams.

The Structure of Dreams

To suppose that dreams in themselves have a regular and definable structure is questionable because in their natural form and as one writes them down or speaks them into a recorder, they often look chaotic and meandering. As one records bits and pieces of a dream, one may suddenly remember some other part, and as one puts it together with the conscious mind, the pieces will take on a kind of form as narrative. But this form is created by consciousness and is not necessarily embedded in the dream as such. But it is helpful nevertheless to consider structure for the purposes of dream interpretation. Jung likens the structure of dreams to classical theater pieces of ancient Greek drama where a scene is set in which some characters appear, a drama begins and develops into a story with emotional tension or conflict, then reaches a climax and concludes with a resolution (lysis). I will consider the following dream from the structural point of view. It was written down by the dreamer a short while after awakening and given to me in this form with permission to use it in this chapter.

I was in the clouds. The sky was pale, almost iridescent blue. I was ascending into the sky on a cloud until I saw an older Japanese man. My cloud stopped just below the one he was sitting on. He was dressed in silk. He gently extended a ring to me. It was clear that this ring was of high value. The ring was made of a gold band with a white pearl in the center. Surrounding the pearl was a circle of irregularly shaped emeralds. One extended out beyond the circle. We did not speak, we communicated telepathically. I asked if he was sure that he wanted me to take the ring. The man indicated that he did. Then I noticed that the ring was quite large on my finger. I looked on the inside of the band and saw the number 8, but it was stamped sideways into the metal, making it appear as an infinity sign. I said, "This is so big, I'm going to need to grow into it." The man smiled and shook his head, almost chuckling; my comment seemed to cause him great amusement. He communicated, "Don't worry."

The first part of the dream structure is the setting, which states where the dream is taking place. In this dream, the location is remarkable and specific: "I was in the clouds."

When people come to a session and tell a dream, they will typically begin by saying something like, "I was at the seashore," or "I was in a house, looking around, and there were some people with me. I think it was my sister, or maybe my wife." Then they begin to tell a story. So at the outset, you get a sense of where you are—"I am in the clouds." The analyst begins imagining the dream with the clients at this point, entering into their dream through the setting. It's important to know where one is when beginning to work with a dream. Being up in the clouds has a very special feeling, and the analyst will take note of that and join the dreamer imaginatively in that dream setting.

The next step is to determine the Dramatis Personae, the cast of characters who make an appearance in the dream. When you go to the theater and buy a program for the performance, which you can read before the play or opera starts, it typically offers a brief description of the place where the drama will begin and gives you a list of characters, the Dramatis Personae. Maybe there are only a few characters, as in a play by Chekhov, or maybe there's a large cast of characters as in Shakespeare's plays. In either case, you get the setting and cast of characters right at the beginning. In a dream report, it's not quite that clear because new characters appear as the story unfolds, but eventually, you can assemble a cast of characters who appear in the dream. One character who will almost certainly show up in the dream is what we call "the dream ego." This is a representation of the dreamer, who speaks as "I," as in the dream above: "I am in the clouds." Most dreams have two or three major characters. In this dream, there are two: the "I" and an older Japanese man. (The dreamer is in her late 30s.) In some dreams, there might be crowds of people, but the significant characters are usually rather small in number.

Then we consider the action in the dream. A narrative begins, and the characters play their parts as the story develops and unfolds. In the dream above, we find the Japanese older man, who is described as elegantly dressed and occupying a cloud nearby and a little higher up than the "I," reaching out to her and giving her a ring, which she accepts, albeit with some questioning and hesitation. A conversation ensues, a message is communicated, and her questions are answered and put to rest by his sense of humor and wise counsel. In this dream, the action is limited and direct. Many dreams that we hear in analytic sessions have much more action, often shifting to other scenes and including complex interactions among the various figures.

Within the action narrative, the dream typically reaches a moment of climax or crisis, or it may show a turning point when the dreamer tells you that suddenly everything changes. This results either in the resolution of the issues depicted in the drama or a break in the dream without a lysis. In our dream, the resolution is clear: The dreamer accepts the ring and a promise of future growth. When dreams show a resolution like this, the dreamer feels closure. The dream process has found a way to solve the problem posed in this case by the ring being too large, and it was able to resolve the question that was building about the size and appropriateness of the gift. Sometimes people wake up before there is a resolution and are left hanging. They don't know how the story ends or how it might come to a conclusion. But a well-formed dream, a complete dream, shows a resolution. It gives the feeling of a completed thought, whether the outcome is fulfillment or tragedy.

In the theater, there is a brief pause at the end of a play after which the actors come out, take a bow, and receive the applause of the audience. The audience will leave the theater with a feeling of having vicariously been through an experience—threatening or beautiful, thrilling or profound. And this is the feeling that one wakes up with after a dream—something has happened, we have had an experience. Sometimes it feels impressive and even numinous as in the dream above, and sometimes it feels like just another little story with no particular meaning. Jung speaks about Big Dreams and little dreams. A Big Dream would give you a feeling of wow! Something really important is taking place in my dream world! That was the effect the dream cited above had on the young woman who reported it.

Working with Dreams in Analysis

Shifting from the structure of dreams, I will now consider more specifically how Jungian psychoanalysts might work with clients on their dreams. If you had gone to C.G. Jung for analysis, he would immediately have asked you for your dreams. Dreams were centrally important for his work with patients. After World War II, when the analyst training programs were set up in Zurich, London, New York, and elsewhere, the curricula universally included personal analysis of candidates. This emphasis on personal analysis has continued to the present day. Students learn about working with dreams in analysis by working with training analysts on their own dreams. However, they also undertake supervision of their cases, and this a second context in which they learn to work with dreams. And then there are didactic courses on the topic of dream analysis. Over the course of training, candidates learn about working with dreams in three different settings: their own personal analysis, the supervision of their clients, and courses on dream analysis.

I trained to become an analyst in Zurich from 1969-73. It was the practice to bring a written copy of our dreams to every single session of analysis, which took place twice per week. We were in training not only to become analysts but also to remember our dreams and to write them down in detail. We would give the analyst a copy of the recent dreams and keep a copy for our own records. This was a routine that we developed and used throughout our training. However, when we started working with clients, we would often run into a problem.

The clients weren't so well trained—they didn't know that they should bring us a copy of their dreams. We had to learn how to elicit dreams from our clients for the analysis. In fact, some clients dream very little, and so one has to be prepared to work analytically in the absence of dreams. But for Jungian psychoanalysis, it's a great advantage to have the access to the unconscious that is provided by dreams. They give us information that the client cannot give from a solely conscious position.

The first step in working with dreams in analysis is to establish the dream text. The client brings in a dream and reads it from a prepared note or retells it from memory. In that moment, the analyst gets a view into the dreamer's unconscious mind. The analyst might ask some questions about the details in the dream. Some analysts spend quite a bit of time on this. For instance, in the case of the dream above, the analyst might ask, "Can you describe the ring in a bit more detail?" and "About how old did the Japanese man look?" The analyst might ask for details about the setting, the environment, and the other characters in the dream.

Once the text has been established and clarified, the second step is to build up a *dream context*, which Jung calls "the tissue in which the dream is embedded." The dream context consists of the client's personal associations to the dream images, memories from the day before the dream occurred (the "day's residue"), and the current life situation of the dreamer. Freud used a method that he called "free association" to work with dreams in psychoanalysis. The dreamer would recall the dream and then associate freely to parts of the dream. The dream was basically interpreted from these associations, more or less leaving the dream itself in the background. This method did not satisfy Jung because he found that free association was repetitious and circled around the same complexes with all dreams. He found that by allowing patients to associate freely in this fashion, they would simply return to the same complexes and obsessions that occupied their waking life. Moreover, the dream itself fell into the background and lost its importance. This wasn't dream interpretation in his view, it was interpretation of the dominant complexes housed in the personal unconscious. He wanted to look at the dream itself as having a message that was original and other and perhaps revelatory of deeper layers of the unconscious. So, he devised a different way of working with dreams. What does the dream want to say? What is it trying to communicate? Jung was much more interested in the message and direction of the dream than in what free associations might tell him.

Jungian psychoanalysts do, however, ask for associations to parts of the dream, but they always come back to the actual dream narrative and images. The associations to each part of the dream are collected one by one. These associations may point to something that has happened very recently. Maybe the dream ends up looking like a commentary on something that happened the day before because the associations all lead there. We have to always keep in mind that a dream comes out of a specific person's life experience. This is "the tissue in which the dream is embedded." In the case of the dream above, the dreamer's association to "Japanese" was "home, a place of safety." This association is a reference to the Caucasian dreamer's safe and secure childhood home, which had been furnished in the Japanese style. Her association to the Japanese man was "ancient wisdom." She had been exposed to Japanese poetry and art during her studies and travels. To the pearl, she had quite a few associations related to her work and to the quality of femininity. Gold and emeralds suggested high quality and value. Such associations will help to create a dream context, which will assist the analyst later to interpret the dream.

Once that step is complete and the personal context in which the dream occurs is established, the next step is *amplification*, which is unique to Jungian analysis. Amplification reaches for the archetypal level of the psyche, which is revealed in dream symbols. It draws parallels from world cultures, religions, mythologies, and fairytales. This is a further level of filling out and deepening the context of the dream. In the case of the dream above, the images of "pearl," "ring," "emeralds," "infinity sign," and "the number 8" would be rich subjects for amplification. The pearl, for instance, is universally associated with the moon and the sea and thus represents the archetypal feminine. Similarly, the emerald is associated with the feminine. A golden ring with the number 8 in the form of the sign for infinity would represent an eternal bonding to the wisdom figure (animus), who brings the gift to the dreamer. Thus, a rich cluster of amplificatory associations is built up around the dream images, which link the dream to the archetypal level of the psyche. This is the purpose of amplification. Amplification is an additional level of association that often comes from the analyst's side because of their extensive training, but not invariably so. The client may also add amplifications to the dream images based on experience and learning. Essentially, dream interpretation is collaborative.

Amplification adds to the context of the dream and can take one far afield into the history of symbols. The focus of analysis and interpretation must then return from the wide fields of amplification to the more narrow and specific aspects of the dream and the dreamer. This going out and return constitutes the hermeneutical circle of dream interpretation.

Now, we come to the final step in the process of working with dreams, and that is the *interpretation* itself. After establishing the text, then gathering personal associations to various aspects of the dream, and amplifying the symbols in the dream, we must ask: What does this dream mean for the dreamer? Why this dream on this night? All that we have done with the dream so far is interesting, but in the end, we have to answer the question of meaning.

Jung proposed a dream theory, and Jungian psychoanalysts draw on this theory to reflect on the meaning of dreams: "... the images in dreams and spontaneous fantasies are symbols, that is, the best possible formulation for still unknown or unconscious facts, which generally compensate the content of consciousness or the conscious attitude."[1] The theory hypothesizes that dreams have a compensatory relationship to consciousness. This dream theory rests on a larger theory of the psyche, which proposes that the psyche seeks equilibrium and balance. It is possible, and indeed typical, that imbalance occurs in the psyche and needs to be redressed. Imbalance comes about because the psyche's components become arranged in a network of polarities, or what Jung called "opposites." The self, which is a term for the psyche as a totality, is then made up of pairs of opposites—masculine/feminine, good/evil, shadow/persona, and so on. Consciousness, as it develops a sense of identity, chooses one side of the opposites to identify with and rejects the other. This creates an imbalance, with consciousness on one side of the divide—a condition that Jung calls one-sidedness—and the unconscious on the other side. Ego-consciousness identifies with and represents one side of the polarities, and the opposite sides are left in the

---

[1] C.G. Jung, *Mysterium Coniunctionis*, CW 14, par. 772.

unconscious. The psyche then has a need to create a state of equilibrium and balance between the opposites. People can be somewhat one-sided and get away with it, but if they are overly so, they become neurotic, suffer severe inner conflicts, and become totally disconnected from important parts of themselves. The net result of this development is that dreams enter as compensation and try to create a better balance.

The theory of compensation states that the dreaming mind serves us by bringing what we need for "wholeness" (aka, balance) and have left out of consciousness. Dreams offer the opportunity to achieve a better balance between the opposites and to create greater equilibrium between ego-consciousness and the unconscious.

Jung was very attracted to the philosophy of Taoism. Within the Tao, Yin and Yang operate on a principle of interplay between the opposites, constantly interacting and affecting each other to form a flow of energy and a direction.

This is a description of the relations between consciousness and the unconscious as the

principle of compensation operates between them.

For interpreting a dream, therefore, it is necessary to know something about the clients' conscious attitudes and sense of identity. One measurement of the situation is typological: Are they extroverted or introverted? Which of the four functions—sensation, intuition, feeling, thinking—is dominant, which secondary? Another measurement is psychological development: Where is the client located in the lifelong trajectory of the individuation process? The dream interpreter needs a clear idea of where the client is one-sided in order to see how the dream is compensating that position. In the case of the person who offered the dream above, the message of the dream would have to do with her present life situation. What she said about the dream was that she felt that the wisdom figure was giving her a "graduation present" for having successfully passed through a difficult midlife crisis. The strong emphasis on the feminine and on commitment seems to suggest a direction for future individuation, which would compensate the dreamer's past identification with the animus side of the syzygy.

It is often difficult to see how a single dream compensates the consciousness of an individual. If there is a dream series available, the meaning of the compensation often becomes more evident.

The person who dreamed of the gift of a ring set with a pearl and emeralds later presented a second dream that underlines the emphasis on the feminine.

I was in a single room made entirely of glass. The room was attached seamlessly to the sheer face of a mountain, the top of which I could not see. I was alone, naked, and quite comfortable. I looked down through the floor of the room and could see trees, ocean, and land. I remember the trees distinctly. I see a glass tub against the far wall of the room filled to the brim with bubbling, warm water. I tumbled into the tub as a child would and began to play in the water. It felt healing, cleansing. An older Japanese man entered the room. I was not at all self-conscious and understood immediately that he was kind, gentle. He walked up to the tub and held up a piece of cloth that was dripping with oil. The sunlight was coming in from outside, and a beam of light was illuminating the cloth and the oil. I remember watching the oil drip into the tub. It was communicated to me that I was to bathe with this oil and that it was the oil of a pink hibiscus. I felt the oil on my skin, the warmth of the sun on my body, and the water swirling around me. Then, an older Japanese woman entered the room. She was carrying a beautiful, delicate bamboo tray. On the tray were plates of delicious-looking food, and pastries —but nothing I recognized or had seen before. She placed the tray silently on the floor next to the tub and smiled at me. The man and the woman then backed out of the room, disappearing into the sheer mountain face.

The dreamer's associations to the dream were to innocence, childhood, and healing. It is a kind of rebirth dream, which Jung referred to as *apoctastasis*, a return to the original state of wholeness. The hibiscus oil again emphasizes the feminine. The second dream helps to specify the area of compensation being addressed: a return to archetypal feminine in order to integrate it more fully into ego-consciousness in the next stages of individuation.

Objective and Subjective Interpretations

Another consideration for dream interpretation is to decide whether it is to be interpreted objectively or subjectively. *Objective* inter-pretation refers meaning to actual relationships in the surrounding world; *subjective* inter-pretation refers meaning to the inner world of the psyche. The dream's compensation can be a response to one-sidedness in one's relationships to other people on the objective level or a response to one's internal one-sidedness on the subjective level. Of course, the two are closely related and, in fact, intertwined, but for analytic purposes, we often make a distinction. The general rule of thumb is that if one dreams about somebody that he or she is in a current relationship with, one would take the dream statement as a response to the present relationship with that person. Otherwise, one would interpret it on the subjective level.

On the objective level, the dream could be suggesting a compensation to help adjust the conscious attitude and behavioral interactions with others, showing the possibility of a more balanced response with less projection. The dream could be indicating a more balanced attitude with less projection. People are generally inclined to think of the familiar people in their dreams as accurate representations of those people, but, of course, they are not. The dream figure is not the objectively real person but rather the dreammaker's portrait of that person. What the dream figure does or says cannot be attributed to the actual person. The dream speaks of the relationship the dreamer has to that figure. Although we say this is an objective interpretation, it still involves the subjective side to a considerable degree.

If the dream is interpreted subjectively, then all parts of the dream, all the figures, and even the dream setting serve as a picture of the dreamer's inner world, with, of course, some reference to the outside world but as metaphor or symbol for an inner psychic reality. The following is a dream of a woman in her 80s, which clearly calls for interpretation on the subjective level but also has reference to a real person albeit long since deceased.

> *A dream in two parts. In the first part, I am observing a group of men (7, I believe) from a position above them. I see them from the waist up. They are known to be exceptionally gifted people, like Mozart. I receive the knowledge that the reason they are gifted is that they are connected to the small circle that is within a larger circle, and this circle is the Source of their genius. Because of this connection, they are able to do what they do. Their magnificent creations are not due to their innate human abilities actually but to their connection to the Source.*
> *In the second part, I am on the same level as the figures, but I see only the feet of the group of men, perhaps the same group. They are wearing remarkable sandals made of silver and gold, and in these, they are able to walk with a fluid movement,*

their feet seemingly smoothly gliding slightly above the ground. I am fascinated by their sandals and movement and think to myself, "This is alchemical!" Then, my father appears and someone says, "He is one of the gifted, but the remarkable thing is that he is so humble. He does not take credit for anything he does or makes happen."

I awake. It is still dark when I get up, and I am convinced that my father is present in the house. Although he died many years ago, he is present here now, or I am in his world with him at this moment.

For this dream, a subjective interpretation is clearly indicated. The dream speaks of the source of creativity (the self) and the union of opposites (silver and gold united in the slippers). It is a marvelous dream for showing the relativization of the ego in favor of the self. The virtue emphasized is humility, the contrary of pride (narcissistic egoism). The dreamer's relation to her father is not being compensated or modified since she has always had a high regard for him. In the dream, he is a symbol of the archetypal Father. The dreamer has historically suffered from the humiliations dealt to daughters by the cultural patriarchy in which she was born and grew up. In patriarchal cultures, fathers assume pride of place and pay little attention to the feminine. The dream father shows the other side of the father figure as a creative personality with the humility to acknowledge a still greater power and source of creativity, the self. As source of creativity, the self would be represented by images like the Great Mother. In this dream, it is simply the circle within a circle, the core of the mandala.

On the subjective level, dreams are taken as symbolic. A symbol is a representation of an unconscious content or process and does not refer to something already known. In this sense, it is different from a sign, which refers to a specific and already known objective object or idea. In general, Jung—and Jungian psychoanalysts who have followed his thinking—are more interested in the symbolic interpretation of dreams than the objective. This is partly because Jung felt that in the modern world, most people are one-sidedly oriented toward the concrete, objective world and have lost touch with the symbolic.

Psychological Type

In working with dreams in analysis, another consideration is psychological type, both of the dreamer and the analyst. It may happen that the client is quite satisfied with merely registering a dream or a fantasy. If the dreamer is a sensation type, he or she will resist going further with interpretation. The dreamer wants to stay with the sensation function within the text of the dream and enjoy the story at its own level. The sensation type will focus on the details of color, texture, place, the quality of the images in the dream and remain content to enjoy it simply at that level. Jung calls this the *aesthetic* attitude. While it is undoubtedly important to gather sensate information in order to establish a text and build up awareness of the images in the dream, the Jungian analyst doesn't want to stop there. This is only the first stage of interpretation.

Others want to use principally the thinking function on their dreams. They approach it abstractly with concepts like ego, shadow, anima, self, compensation, and so forth. When they have understood the dream in this fashion, they are satisfied and think they have done the work of interpretation. Thinking types will immediately jump to the stage of interpretation to see how the dream compensates consciousness, and in this way they overlook details and neglect to ask further important questions that would come up by using feeling and intuition. Of these two options, Jung writes:

> It often happens that the patient is quite satisfied with merely registering a dream or fantasy, especially if he has preten- sions to *aestheticism*. He will then fight against ... *intellectual understanding* because it seems an affront to the reality

of his psychic life. Others try to understand with their brains only, and want to
skip the ... practical stage. And when
they have understood, they think they
have done their full share of realization.[2]

The feeling function introduces the question
of the value of the dream in the dreamer's life.
Does the dreamer have a feeling relationship to
the contents of the unconscious? It is the feeling
function that binds the dream to values and
brings an ethical dimension to the work with
dreams. What ethical issues does the dream raise
for the dreamer? Interestingly, Freud confronted
himself with serious ethical matters as a result of
analyzing his own dreams in *Interpretation of
Dreams*. His reflection on his dreams was a
coming-to-consciousness of hidden motives and
shadow impulses that were unconscious to him
in waking life.

People often think of ethics as a simple
matter of following rules and codes of conduct
that govern a particular area of life—business,
marital relations, politics, etc. Every profession
has ethical codes and rules that instruct the
members in general how to conduct themselves
correctly. Infractions are punished by courts.
What we mean, however, by attending to the
values brought to awareness by the feeling

---

[2] C.G. Jung "The Psychology of the Transference," CW 16, par. 489.

function is different from obedience to objective codes of behavior. It brings conscience into the picture. The feeling function in Jung's formulation is a rational function that has to do with values. It is thinking with the heart, not the head, as Blaise Pascal wrote: "The heart has its reasons which reason knows nothing of. ... We know the truth not only by the reason, but by the heart." Jung writes:

> That they should have a *feeling-relationship* to the contents of the unconscious seems strange to them or even ridiculous. ... Feeling always binds one to the reality and meaning of symbolic contents, and these in turn impose binding standards of ethical behaviour from which aestheticism and intellectualism are only too ready to emancipate themselves. ... The alchemists thought that the opus demanded not only laboratory work, the reading of books, meditation, and patience, but also love. Nowadays we would speak of 'feeling-values' and of realization through *feeling.*[3]

The feeling type is a person who functions on the basis not of ideas but of certain values— justice, compassion, decency toward others, fairness to oneself, etc. Using the feeling function,

---

[3] *Ibid.*

dream interpretation takes up the ethical implications of the dream. That means not only enjoying the dream for its beauty or intelligence, but for its ethical message and ultimately its practical meaning for how one lives. The feeling function contributes to integrating the practical meaning of the dream. In the dream of the golden ring (above), the feeling function would consider how the dreamer will need to grow into the relationship implied by receiving the ring, namely to take up the ethical task of love. The dream offers vocational direction.

Finally, there is also the function of intuition that needs to come into play when considering the meaning of a dream. On this point, Jung writes:

> Nor is realization through feeling the final stage. … The fourth stage is the anticipation of the lapis. The imaginative activity of the fourth function—intuition, without which no realization is complete—is plainly evident in this anticipation of a possibility whose fulfilment could never be the object of empirical experience at all. … Intuition gives outlook and insight; it revels in the garden of magical possibilities as if they were real. … This keystone rounds off the

work into an experience of the totality of the individual.[4]

The intuitive function looks ahead toward the future and considers the question of where the dream is tending. What is its goal, psychologically considered? Jung uses the phrase "imaginative activity" for working with the intuitive function. Active imagination is employed on the dream to carry it into a space where one can consider its trajectory into the unknown future. How could this dream apply to various life situations which one may experience in the future? Imagination expands and extends the range of possible meanings that the dream might have for the dreamer's life. Jung also uses the phrase "the garden of magical possibilities" as the place where intuition can lead us.

The Dream Series in Analysis

When a person comes into analysis, the analyst will ask the client if he or she has had any dreams to discuss. In addition, the analyst will typically encourage the client to keep a dream notebook or journal as the analysis proceeds. This is how a dream series begins to get built up. One can see the result in the dream series of Wolfgang Pauli, which Jung interprets in *Psychology and Alchemy*.

---

[4] *Ibid.*, par. 492.

As clients get more involved with their dream life and begin recording the dreams regularly, sometimes they remember earlier dreams from childhood or recurrent dreams that have repeated themselves over and over again, and these, too, become part of the dream series.

In analysis, before a dream series emerges, the analyst receives what is called the "initial dream." The initial dream is handled with particular interest and respect. It is often the case that when one looks back over the history of a case, one can see all the major issues and themes presented in an early form in the initial dream. One can think of the initial dream as a gift to the analyst—it is saying, "Here is what we are going to be working with as we engage with this psyche." Dreams that follow the initial dream week to week, month to month, and over the course of the entire analysis, form the contents of the dream series.

When analysts receive dreams in the sessions, they place them in the context of the dreams that have come before. After a while, themes emerge and figures reappear, and the series shows the client's individuation process unfolding through this period of time. Jung discovered that dreams in a series do not just repeat exactly the same problems and outcomes over and over again but rather show progress and development. Jung thought of this development as being instigated by the instinct for individuation, which drives the psyche to unfold, integrate, develop, and become what it potentially can be.

Jung put forward a second and, we might say, supplementary theory about the unconscious. The first theory was that the unconscious compensates consciousness, especially the one-sidedness of consciousness. The second theory is that the unconscious has a goal, which he called "prospective." The unconscious has a direction that is aimed toward the development of the personality. This is the individuation instinct. Dreams facilitate this process. The single acts of compensation are in the service of the psyche's *telos*, namely full realization of potential.

Pillar Four

Active Imagination as Agent of Transformation

The important role of active imagination in Jungian analysis was established by Jung himself, and its centrality was rooted in his personal experience. This was partially described in Chapter Six of *Memories, Dreams, Reflections* titled "Confrontation with the Unconscious." The title of this chapter indicates the role active imagination plays in coming to terms with the split in the psyche between ego-consciousness and identity on the one hand and the instinctual and archetypal forces of the unconscious. The full story of how Jung used active imagination in his confrontation is told in *The Red Book: Liber Novus*, which was published only in 2009, nearly a century after its creation. In Jung's practice with patients, active imagination took a central role because of its effectiveness as an agent of transformation. Combined with working with dreams in analysis, active imagination proved to be crucial for achieving the maximum therapeutic impetus toward facilitating the client's individuation. The container for this process is the analytic relationship (the temenos), as I have discussed earlier.

To begin this explication of active imagination as a method of treatment, a brief description of what it is will be helpful. Active imagination is a form of self-engagement, and it requires the intentional introversion of psychic energy. In active imagination, the direction of one's attention, focus, thoughts, and feelings is turned inward to images that might occur. Extroversion directs a person's attention to the world around, introversion to the world within. Typically, most of a person's day is spent in the extroverted mode attending to things in the world around. But sometimes this shifts. If you go to a concert, for instance, and listen to the music carefully and with full attention, what you are aware of is actually the vibrations in the air that are coming into your ears and being translated into brain waves. Your attention is to the sounds that are coming to you from the outside. Sometimes, however, when you're listening to music, you might start seeing images in your mind's eye, in your inner world, or you might see colors or some kinds of movement. This is called synesthesia. Or you might start having fantasy images of a landscape or of people you know. If you start paying attention to what is going on in your mind, you're changing modes from extra-version to introversion. Extroversion is listening to the sounds, and introversion is looking at how the sounds are affecting you. In your inner world, the music is creating emotion, images, or thoughts.

Dreaming is pure introversion. While dreaming, one is experiencing the inner world exclusively. This is a realm of pure representation. Some philosophies argue that, in fact, we only experience our inner world, and what we take to be the outer world is a mental construction pure and simple. In psychology, however, there is a strong conviction that our senses and mental functions do give us an impression, perhaps not altogether accurate, of an external world. We make a distinction between inner world and outer world, although it is recognized that the two are entangled and often very difficult to separate because of projection. Active imagination is a deliberate turning inward in an attempt to engage the psyche's subjectivity as deeply as possible while in a waking state. It is a kind of meditation.

We can draw some comparisons between dreaming (see previous chapter) and active imagination. Active imagination is similar to dreaming, only it is carried out while the subject is awake and fully conscious and therefore has control over the frame. Dreaming is the brain thinking, but in images and stories rather than logically. Active imagination is very much like this, using images and stories rather than directed thinking. In dreams, we speak of a dream-ego, which participates actively or passively in the narrative. In active imagination, the subject-ego may also be active or passive, but it is by choice. The subject chooses to be actively engaged in the imagined drama taking place or may choose to be a quiet observer, but even as an observer, the subject is active in the sense that it is by active choice and not merely passive watching as in daydreaming. When Jung writes about active imagination, he stresses the word *active* in order to distinguish it from passive fantasy. Both words in active imagination are important—it is imagination and also active, not passive.

Jung's Discovery of Active Imagination

It is useful to look at the history and development of active imagination and at how Jung came upon this method, used it for himself, and then applied it in his clinical work with patients. Shortly before Jung broke off his relationship with Freud, he wrote a book titled *Symbols and Transformations of the Libido,* which later in a revised version became *Symbols of Transformation,* Vol. 5 of his *Collected Works.* In this book, Jung discussed and analyzed a series of fantasies of a young woman named Frank Miller, an American who was traveling in Europe for a period of time. Jung became interested in this material, which he found published in a Swiss journal, and he did a great deal of research into the psychological background of these fantasies. Basically, he amplified the images of Miss Miller using mythology from many different traditions and parts of the world. He also studied a broad spectrum of literature in order to amplify the deeper meanings of these passive fantasies that Frank Miller had produced in her journal.

In the first chapter of *Symbols and Transformations of the Libido,* Jung writes about two types of thinking, fantasy thinking and directed thinking. Fantasy thinking is what he discovered in Miller's journal, whereas directed thinking is the more logical, rational, and scientific that Jung used in his discussion of the material. He was trained as a scientist and medical doctor, so when he began his research he assumed that directed thinking was far superior to fantasy thinking. Fantasy thinking was considered immature, like what children do when playing. They play with toys and make up stories, pretend that they are a character different from themselves, and generally engage in fantasy thinking. This is generally considered to be childish compared to the directed, logical thinking of adults. Jung then reflected further on the meaning of fantasies and studied them from a deeper psychological perspective, which he would later call an archetypal perspective. He came to a new appreciation and indeed became fascinated by fantasy thinking as he began to understand its deeper level. In fact, it expresses a kind of truth that directed thinking is not capable of reaching, a type of psychological truth.

Shortly after the publication of that book, he and Freud ended their personal relationship, and Jung resigned from his positions in the International Psychoanalytic Association. Jung states in *Memories, Dreams, Reflections* that at this time in his life (he was 37-38 years old), he felt disoriented and didn't know what direction to take in his life and professional career. He knew that directed thinking and trying to figure it out rationally would not be of much help, so he decided to try an experiment and do what Miss Miller had done, namely to play and to engage with fantasy thinking. What is it like to think and yet not use the ego's directed thinking function to rationally solve a problem? This was his first question. This experiment became a major turning point that Jung had not anticipated. He discovered active imagination as an agent of transformation. He had set out to discover for himself what it means to think with imagination, and he discovered himself.

This experiment was preceded by a number of important dreams that Jung had in the months leading up to his active imagination experiment. He surmised that by using his imagination, he could unlock the meaning of these dreams that he had not been able to interpret using rational methods. Jung begins the story by recalling a dream he had a year or so before beginning the fantasy experiment. In the dream, he's sitting at a round table in his home, and suddenly, a white bird enters the room, sits on the table, and then magically turns into a little girl. Jung is fascinated. She is very charming, so he speaks to her. Then suddenly, she turns back into a white bird and flies out the window and disappears. When he asks someone in the dream: "Where did the little girl go? Where does she live, that white bird?" the answer came back, "She lives in the land of the dead." Jung didn't understand what this meant. Who is this little girl that's also a bird? Where is the land of the dead? What does this all mean?

A year later, in November 1913, Jung made the decision to spend some time in his study every evening after his day's work and dinner with his family in his home in Kusnacht. He put aside a particular time to sit in his study and concentrate on this experiment, using fantasy thinking to see where it would lead. He started by opening his mind and, in his imagination, calling out the window overlooking Lake Zurich: "My soul where are you? Do you hear me? I speak, I call you—are you there? I have returned. I am here again. I have shaken the dust of all the lands from my feet, and I have come to you. I am with you. After long years of long wandering, I have come to you again."[1] He then simply sat there, maybe an hour or two every evening for several months, and let his imagination explore the inner world that opened up to him. He wanted to find "the land of the dead," his soul, the hidden depths of the psyche. His imagination led him to discover for himself the answers he sought. Active imagination is an experience, and the knowledge that is acquired by using this method is what might be called Gnosis.

At first, the way inward was very slow and difficult for Jung. For several nights, nothing happened and nothing appeared in his imagination. He waited somewhat impatiently. During this period, as Jung wrote in his notebooks (the Black Books), it was as though he were in the desert—dry and barren—and nothing appeared when he called out to his soul. There was no activity at all. Fortunately, he persisted and continued to wait. Finally, a figure whom he calls his soul speaks to him. Only on the 12th night, he writes, "The spirit of the depths opened my eyes and I caught a

---

[1] C.G. Jung, *The Red Book: Liber Novus*, Reader's Edition, p. 127.

glimpse of the inner things, the world of my soul."[2] It was a matter of endurance, like journeying through the desert.

Looking around in this space of his imagination, he finds himself on the floor of a cave, ankle-deep in mud. Now he could become active by exploring the interior of the cave. This is the beginning of his *active* imagination. As he looks around, he sees a luminous red stone sitting on top of a rock. He approaches to take a closer look, and as he does so, he begins to hear voices shrieking. As he takes the crystal in his hand, he sees a hole in the rock and peers into the Underworld. He hears a stream of rushing water deep under the surface of the cave. Jung is astonished by the sounds and images and is surprised by what is happening in his imagination. (Surprise is a very important feature of active imagination—something happens that the subject does not expect. The ego is not in charge, and the unconscious images are showing autonomy.) As Jung peers into the depths, he sees something very disturbing: the bloody head of a man, and a dead body is floating in the water. He then sees a large dark scarab and a radiant sun shining up through the dark waters. Blood suddenly starts pouring out of the hole. Jung had no idea what this experience meant or how to

---

[2] *Ibid.*, p. 147.

interpret it. He simply made a record in his journal, writing down everything he saw, thought, and felt. But the meaning was unclear to him. Yet from his studies of mythology, he knew that this was part of the process that is classically called a Nekyia, a journey to the Underworld. The parallel between the psychological descent into the unconscious using active imagination and the mythological accounts of the journey to the Underworld is obvious.

We have to keep in mind when reading *Liber Novus* that Jung didn't have a professional guide to reassure him or shed light on the meaning of the process he was undergoing. In fact, he was quite alone and at times became worried about where this experiment was taking him. Would he end up with a mental breakdown? Would he "throw a schizophrenia?" he wondered anxiously. He was an experienced psychiatrist and had seen what mental illness looks like. So, he worried about the possibility of a latent psychosis lurking in his unconscious that might burst through the walls of his ego-consciousness and render him temporarily incapable of functioning. He had seen patients in the hospital with the kind of fantasies he was experiencing in his private office. It was a serious concern.

On the other hand, he was pleased that his imagination was working, that something was happening, and that he was being surprised. His imagination was becoming interesting and alive. Reflecting on his options, he decided to continue his experiment.

A week after his visit to the cave, he comes upon a scene in which he meets two figures: an old man who looks like one of the ancient prophets and a beautiful young woman who is blind. They are accompanied by a black serpent. With this encounter, the first major story in *Liber Novus* unfolds. The prophet introduces himself as Elijah and the woman as Salome. Jung is astonished, and a fascinating narrative develops over the course of their interactions and conversations that follow. The episode lasts for five sessions of active imagination, December 21-25, 1913. Jung discovers that they also live in the Land of the Dead, which is where the girl in his earlier dream was from and which he had set out to find when he began his experiment with imagination. This territory is what he would call in his theoretical writings on psychology, "the unconscious." It is where myths come from. He has found the source, and he is discovering his personal myth.

Who are these two people? Salome and Elijah are biblical figures, so they've long since been dead, and yet they are still very much alive in this land where they currently live. Jung is discovering that the Land of the Dead is cultural history and now a part of the collective unconscious. That long-ago past is still alive and active within the psyche. This would lead him to argue that in the unconscious time does not exist as it does in consciousness. The distinction among past, present, and future breaks down in the unconscious. Everything is present at once. As we observe Jung's behavior and how he interacts with these figures, we see that he remains himself an educated European man of the 20th century. He remains very much himself in his questioning, arguing, and thinking. He doesn't become fictionalized or different from his usual waking personality. In his active imagination, he is engaging with figures who, while they are a part of himself in the sense of belonging to his inner world, yet are unfamiliar to him and represent attitudes and viewpoints other than his conscious ones. In *Liber Novus*, we can observe how Jung, as he practices active imagination over several years, gradually undergoes a profound transformation. Not only does he change and evolve, however, but the figures with which he interacts also evolve. There is a mutual transformation process going on in which all parts of the psyche are affected because of the dialogue and the interaction taking place between them.

At a certain point, Jung was so impressed by what was happening to him inwardly that he decided to create what we now know as the Red Book, which he titled *Liber Novus* (*The New Book*).

Jung thought deeply and over a long period of time about the meaning of his active imagination narrative. Besides reflecting on the psychological meaning for himself personally, he also introduced active imagination as a therapeutic method to his patients. In 1916, some three years after he began his experiment, he delivered a paper to his students and colleagues at the Psychology Club titled "The Transcendent Function." There, he describes the practice of active imagination and presents the result of this work as the construction of a bridge between ego-consciousness and the unconscious. The meaning of "transcendent" in this term is that it rises above the abyss between the two sides of the psyche. The "transcendent function" allows the conscious mind to go beyond the limits of directed rational thinking and connects the ego to another realm of the psyche, thereby delivering what could be called intuitive knowledge, or "gnosis." Jung came to realize that directed thinking cannot connect the ego to the unconscious. It can study the effects of the unconscious, as Jung and his colleagues did in the Word Association Studies and as Freud did in his psychoanalysis, but its range of experience is limited to consciousness. Active imagination can take the subject further into what Henry Corbin, following Jung and expanding on the topic of active imagination from his studies in Sufism, called the *Mundus Imaginalis*.

Active Imagination in Jungian Psychoanalysis

Imagine going to Jung for analysis, stepping into his office, and meeting him. The first session is introductory: You tell your story, list your complaints and problems, and Jung listens carefully but does not say much. Then, he encourages you to do two things before you come to the next session: to record your dreams and to begin practicing active imagination. If he said this to you, it would be a real compliment—he would be estimating that you are capable of doing this inner work. He would have made a very quick evaluation and diagnosis of your psychological stability and capacity. By the end of the session, he is in effect saying, "You are ready to work and do analysis with me." This would begin an extraordinary period of working in introversion.

You would be engaged in a lot of work between sessions if you were in analysis with Jung. It isn't only taking place in the hour of analysis; it's ongoing, intensive work between the hours of analysis. Jung worked in this way with most of his patients in his later life. His clients were mostly mature people, some of them well advanced into the second half of life. If he worked with you in this thoroughly engaged way, he would be assuming that you did not need to do the work that's so necessary in the first half of life: building a persona, getting into your life, and becoming independent of your family of origin, creating a strong ego. He would assume that you've done that already. Many people who worked with Jung in analysis would go into this type of total immersion for a relatively short period of time. They would come to Zurich and do analysis with him for a couple of months and then return home. Many of his patients lived in other countries. While they were with him, they exerted themselves intensively in an introverted way in order to experience and build up an inner world by making contact with figures of the unconscious through working with their dreams and engaging in active imagination. It was a very special time in their lives as Jung assisted and guided them in the discovery of their inner depths.

Once they were advanced in active imagination and working with their dreams, they could carry on these activities without necessarily having to be in analysis. After they left their residency in Switzerland and went back home, the work they began with Jung could continue. Active imagination helped them to become in-dependent of the analyst. It facilitated an ongoing process. They had developed certain skills and the ability to be in a creative and fruitful relationship with their unconscious independently. Typically, Jung's patients would begin their active imagination work when they came to see him and then continue doing it perhaps for the rest of their lives, perhaps returning to see him occasionally.

During these reunions with Jung, they might review some of the experiences they had in the meantime. But Jung felt that learning to do active imagination freed them from the transference and from dependency on him. It gave them the ability to continue their inner work on their own, when they were not actively in analysis with him.

Joseph Henderson, an American, came to Zurich as a young man in the 1920s and worked with Jung for a period of time. After he finished his training, which took place between Zurich and London, he moved to San Francisco and eventually founded the Jung Institute there with his friend and colleague Joseph Wheelwright. Joseph Henderson once told me a bit about his experience in Kusnacht. He stayed in a hotel not far from Jung's home and office. He walked to Jung's home for his sessions several times a week. In the early morning, he said, he would come out on the hotel terrace and see other people sitting there working on their dreams and doing active imagination. He said that's how you could tell which of the hotel guests were working with Jung. If they were sitting on the terrace writing in their journals, painting a picture, or even with their eyes closed and obviously doing active imagination, they were Jung's patients! These people were preparing for their afternoon or evening analytic session with Jung. Henderson told me that it was inconceivable to work with

Jung and not be engaged in active imagination. It was a basic method for analysis.

That's how active imagination became one of the four pillars of Jungian psychoanalysis. It's foundational for the work of contacting the unconscious, building the transcendent function, and creating a bridge between the conscious and unconscious parts of the psyche.

Jung discusses several analytic cases in his published writings and seminars that include extensive active imagination content. In *The Visions Seminar,* he looks at the active imagination material of Christiana Morgan, an American woman who came for sessions in the 1920s and later returned to Boston, where, with Henry Murray, she created the Thematic Apperception Test (TAT). He devotes a major section of his book *Psychology and Alchemy* to a series of dreams and active imaginations by the physicist Wolfgang Pauli, who came to him for analysis in the 1930s. And he writes a major essay titled "A Study in the Individuation Process" on the active imaginations and paintings of Dr. Kristine Mann, an American psychiatrist who came to study with him in the 1920s and continued with intermittent frequency until her death in the 1940s.

As an example of the therapeutic effects of active imagination, the case of Wolfgang Pauli is instructive. Pauli was a professor at ETH Zurich, where Jung was also a professor at the time. His father, who was a professor in Vienna, suggested that he consult with Professor Jung about the troubles he was having in his personal life. Pauli realized that he needed help, so he came to Jung for analysis. Jung interviewed him and decided it would be better if he began by working with a female student of his because Pauli was having a lot of difficulties in his relationships with women. Secondly, both Pauli and Jung were professors at the same university, and it probably would have been difficult to separate roles. So, Jung referred him to Dr. Erna Rosenbaum, who took over the analysis of Pauli. He was in analysis with Rosenbaum for some nine months, during which time he produced an impressive series of dreams and active imaginations, which he then offered to Jung for his research purposes. It is these that Jung analyzes in his commentary. After his analysis with Rosenbaum, he continued in analysis with Jung for some 18 months, after which their relationship changed and continued in the form of correspondence and occasional meetings to discuss theoretical topics and occasionally Pauli's dreams.

About 18 years later, in 1953, Pauli produced a paper called "The Piano Lesson," which is an active imagination of about 10 pages in length. It shows Pauli creating a balance and harmony between two parts within himself. In this active imagination, he finds a way to bring together his rational, scientific, and brilliant intelligence with his emotional life, with his anima world and the unconscious. He uses the metaphor of the piano with white and black keys working together to create a single piece of music. It could be said that through the use of active imagination and working with his dreams, Pauli was able to achieve a very considerable level of balance and integration of the opposites. It was this inner harmony that was crucial for his life and for his work.

Jung found Pauli's dreams and active imagination material fascinating because Pauli was such a gifted man, committed to recording his dreams in detail, and exceptional at working with his images and visions. He was dedicated to active imagination, as the record shows. In Pauli's case, we can see how dreams and active imaginations move together in a steady and clear direction toward what Jung called the synthesis of the psyche and the development of a transcendent function. One of the things that Pauli realized as a result of his analysis was how therapeutically the work affected his life. As long as he stayed in contact with his unconscious by observing his dreams and working in active imagination, he felt emotionally stable, enriched, and balanced. He continued doing this for the rest of his life.

Dr. Kristine Mann presents a complementary case. She was an American woman who came to

Jung for analysis in the 1920s, when she was about 55 years old. Mann was an accomplished single professional woman, a psychiatrist with a practice in New York City, who felt a need to work with her unconscious in a different way than had been available to her. She felt stuck. She came to Jung hoping to find a way forward in her life and her individuation process. Jung comments on about 20 pictures that Mann painted while in analysis with him and afterward in "A Study in the Process of Individuation," which was published after her death.

The first picture that she brought to Jung when she came to him for analysis shows a woman stuck in rocks. The second picture shows a lightning strike, which frees a boulder from the rocks. Release and freedom from oppression are represented in this picture. Mann practiced active imagination by painting. This is one of the ways that active imagination can be done: hand to paper with a brush, putting the images on a surface so they can be seen instead of holding them in imagination. When Mann brought these pictures to Jung, they would discuss them as products of active imagination. She would tell him what they meant to her and how they came about. At one point, she said that she had decided not to follow "reason" but to let her "eyes" lead the way and tell her how the images would be presented.

In this way, she would be surprised by the picture that emerged.

The picture series that she produced while working with Jung over some 10 years represents her individuation process in images. When she returned to New York after working with Jung for several months in Switzerland, she continued her paintings. She returned to Switzerland in the summers and resumed her work with Jung for several weeks. Over the course of about 20 years, she produced a series of beautiful paintings, many of them in the form of mandalas. Jung writes in his commentary on these pictures that he sees the process of individuation moving forward step by step through these images made in her active imagination paintings. Her process was done through color and form, mainly abstract images. This was her form of active imagination, and it was transformative.

Precautions for the Use of Active Imagination in Analysis

There are a number of precautions one needs to take as an analyst before introducing a client to active imagination. One has to be aware of the psychological condition of the person that one is seeing and to make a careful evaluation of his or her level of development and level of psycho-pathology. Active imagination can become a very powerful and disruptive method because it stimulates the unconscious, and images emerge in the process that can be disturbing, as one can see clearly in Jung's *Liber Novus*. If the ego isn't strong enough to contain the affects released and work with the images as they emerge, the client can become overwhelmed by what Jung called latent psychosis. Analysts will typically work with their clients for a period of time before they decide whether it's appropriate to introduce active imagination as a method. With some clients, one would never use it either because of psychopathology or lack of sufficient ego development or inappropriate timing, given what is happening in the client's life at the time.

Another rule in active imagination is not to use known persons as active imagination characters. In other words, one should not do active imagination with somebody one knows as a friend, a colleague, or a loved one because it can have unusual effects. It would be a misuse of active imagination to try to influence other people through a type of "magical intervention" unknown by them. Using active imagination in that way violates the limits of ethical practice and behavior with regard to other people. If by chance a known person pops up in active imagination, the advice is to find a replacement for that person as a representative of an inner figure that he or she might resemble. For instance, Mr. Z is someone whom I find distasteful and is a kind of shadow figure for me. If he comes into my active imagination, I recognize him and try to find a similar imaginal character to represent the same shadow qualities. I can then go ahead and dialogue with him.

Types of Active Imagination

There are a variety of modes one can use in active imagination. The instructions below could be called the classical form: You create a clear space in your mind, wait for whatever appears, if it moves follow it, and so on. This is the classic form of active imagination as developed by Jung. Then, there is the modality that Kristine Mann used: drawing and painting. Some people use clay modeling or sculpting. There is also active imagination in movement, where the body leads the way in active imagination. This is practiced by some Jungian analysts and is called "authentic movement." And then, of course, there is sand play, which is practiced by many therapists worldwide. For this, one places miniature objects in a tray of sand and creates a scene from which a narrative emerges.

Starting Points for Active Imagination

Active imagination can start in a variety of ways. It can begin with a dream. If a dream is unfinished upon awakening, or if there is something in the dream that the dreamer would like to explore further, or if there is a figure in the dream to engage with further, active imagination can be used to dream the dream onward.

Active imagination may also begin with a mood or a feeling. If you were going to make a movie to represent this feeling, what would it be about, and what role would you play? Starting with a feeling or a mood, perhaps in imagination you find yourself alone beside a lake and someone comes toward you—you engage that person in dialogue.

Some Tips for Practicing of Active Imagination

To begin, there is a starting point, a first session. One needs to make a quiet and free mental space for imagination. As I have said, active imagination is not daydreaming or a matter of falling into a fantasy that pops into consciousness. Active imagination is a deliberate undertaking, and one has to prepare for it. Begin by setting aside 30 minutes in a physical place free of outside disturbance: no telephone calls, no messages, no conversation.

Tip # 1: Let It Happen! (*Geschehenlassen, Wu Wei*)

The first rule is simple: Just let it happen. In German, the word to describe this type of activity is the verb, *geschenlassen*. When Jung studied and commented on the Chinese alchemical text "The Secret of the Golden Flower," he discovered that this has an equivalent in the Chinese language: *wu wei*. It's a type of active passivity: active in that it is a choice made by the awake subject (the ego), passive in that it means "do nothing, wait." This is the first instruction Jung received from his soul. She whispered to him, "Wait." It's a simple instruction, but it can be agonizing to carry out: "I heard the cruel word. Torment belongs to the desert,"[3] Jung writes in *Liber Novus*.

At first, you might have to wait patiently for quite a time until something starts to happen in your imagination. It is not easy to empty the busy mind of the thoughts that preoccupy it. It's a discipline. Spurious thoughts keep intruding, and it's a challenge to let them go. The idea is to create a blank screen in your mind in which you're thinking of nothing, seeing nothing, feeling nothing—it's just empty space. In some forms of

---

[3] *Ibid.*, p. 141.

meditation, this is the final goal. For active imagination, it's the beginning, a prerequisite.

To do this, it's helpful if your body is relaxed. In some meditation practices, people sit on a cushion with their legs crossed or folded. There is also the so-called walking meditation. The main thing is to calm your conscious mind, to empty it of its concerns and preoccupations. When complexes, worries, or thoughts from everyday life intrude, just let them go and clear the space. This is what we see Jung doing at the beginning of *Liber Novus*. Simply and patiently wait for something to appear, not forcing it, not trying to summon an image. This is the initial session. Later, there will be a change in how to begin a session of active imagination, but at the beginning, start with emptiness.

Dr. Marie-Louise von Franz, who was one of Jung's outstanding students and wrote a good deal about active imagination, including a book titled *Alchemical Active Imagination,* once told the story of a client whom she advised to do some active imagination. She gave him the basic instructions as outlined above, and when the client came to her for his session the next week, she asked: "Did you do the exercise?" He replied: "I tried, but nothing happened. Nothing came to me. I didn't see anything." She suggested he try again the following week: "Do the same thing. Clear your mind, make an empty space and wait.

See what comes to you." The next week the report was the same. He said he tried to do the active imagination and sat quietly for half an hour. He waited, cleared his mind, but nothing came. This went on for weeks and weeks, and it was always the same story. He was a very patient man, so he continued faithfully to try. Then, one week he came in really excited and said: "I saw something!" She asked, "What did you see?" He said he was sitting quietly as usual in front of his window at home when, all of a sudden, he saw the image of a goat outside the window. The goat was just standing there and looking off into the distance. She said, "That's great. Now it's begun." He told her that he didn't like goats very much, and he wished it had been something else. Dr. von Franz said, "Just stay with what you see."

Tip # 2: Receive Whatever Comes.

This brings us to the second rule. The first rule is letting go and clearing a space; and the second rule is to *receive whatever comes*.

Dr. von Franz's client would rather have had something more interesting than a goat. He lived in the countryside of Switzerland where goats are rather common and not very interesting. Maybe he would rather have seen an eagle or a mountain lion. But he was instructed to stay with what came to him. This is an essential rule. We can remember Jung's experience from *The Red Book* where he describes going into the cave and seeing something horrible, something he would not have invited or wanted in any way. Yet he had to accept what was offered in his imagination. We all have an inner editor; an attitude or judge of what's noble, what's base, what's worthy, and what's unworthy. We have to put that editor aside and simply receive whatever comes—the first thing that arrives and reveals itself in the imagination.

This rule sets active imagination apart and makes it different from meditation practices that have a program or guided imagery. For instance, in guided meditation, you may begin by thinking about a particular scene from a particular text, and in the second meditation, you may meditate on a particular figure or deity. There are instructions for each of these. Active imagination is not like this. Once you've made yourself comfortable, cleared your mind of distracting thoughts, and something appears to you in your space of imagination, don't judge it. Just receive it, accept it, and stay with it.

This is the instruction that von Franz gave to her client. She said, "You've seen a goat outside the window? Stay with it—what does it do? Watch it. Pay attention and see what happens." When the client came back the next week for his session, she asked him what happened. The client said that nothing happened, the goat just stayed where he was the week before. She again encouraged him saying, "Well, stay with it during the week, keep doing it every day, watch him, stay with the image, see what happens." He came back the following week, and it was the same story—nothing happened. This went on for weeks and weeks. He was patient and kept looking out the window—the goat was still there. But nothing happened beyond that.

Then suddenly in the middle of the night, von Franz's phone rang, and she picked up the receiver. It was this client on the other end of the line. "Dr. von Franz, I'm going crazy! You have to admit me to the mental hospital. I'm losing my mind." She said to him on the phone: "Can you wait till the morning? I'll see you early. Come to my office at 7:00 a.m. We'll have an emergency session. You can tell me what's happening, and we'll see if you need to be hospitalized. I'll take care of it. But can you wait until morning?" He said he would wait. When he arrived at 7:00 the next morning, she let him into her consulting room. "What happened? What's the matter? Tell me what's going on." He said when he was doing his active imagination yesterday, looking out the window as usual, he saw the head of the goat. All of a sudden, the goat moved his head and looked right at him. "I'm sure I'm going crazy. I can't control my mind. That goat is just doing whatever it wants." Von Franz laughed and said that's what is supposed to happen in active imagination.

"Now you have something happening and you can interact with that goat. Active imagination is beginning now."

Tip #3: If It Moves, Follow It

This introduces the third rule of active imagination. *If it moves, follow it* and stay with that movement in the imagination. This brings in not only the rule of acceptance—staying with whatever comes—but it also brings in the rule of the active ego engaging with autonomous figures in the imagination, which seem to have a life and will of their own. In this stage of active imagination, it's important that the ego, the "I" in the story, maintains its usual attitudes and feelings. Subjects need to enter the story that's developing with the full reality of who they are and act as though the dialogue and scene is really happening in front of them. That's the difference between active imagination and passive fantasy. In passive fantasy, you just watch what's happening. In active imagination, you enter into it and engage with it as though it were a real, physical, dramatic event happening in front of you and around you.

Jung tells the story of a patient, a young man, who came to him with an account of an active imagination he had done between sessions. The young man said that in his active imagination, he was with his fiancée who was skating on the ice of a nearby lake. He was standing at the edge of the lake watching. Suddenly, the ice broke, and she fell into the ice-cold water and was screaming for help, and it looked as if she were drowning. Jung exclaimed, "Oh no! What did you do?" The young man admitted with embarrassment that he just stood passively and watched the scene in front of him as if it were a movie. Jung asked, "What would you do if this was really happening?" He said that if it were really happening, he would call for help and would jump into the water to try to save her. Jung said: "Well, that's exactly what you should do in active imagination. Be yourself as much as you possibly can, as you would be if this event were taking place in the physical world around you." The point is that there is strong ego-involvement in active imagination. This is not passive fantasy. The ego allows the story to unfold, but at the same time, the subject is also an actor in the scene that's being played out in the imagination.

These are the basic rules of active imagination: Let go and empty the mind; receive whatever comes; if it moves follow it; and then interact genuinely with it. If you follow these basic rules, you're sure to have success in practicing active imagination.

If you wish to try active imagination, follow these rules. Set aside 20 to 30 minutes every day for a week and make an attempt to begin active imagination. You can set a timer, and after about 20 minutes of practicing your active imagination, write down in a journal exactly what happened. The next day, pick up where you left it the day before. Go back into the scene and continue from there. If you do this regularly for a month, you will have the beginning of a stable inner world that you can visit and receive the benefits of active imagination for the rest of your life. This sounds like a big promise; it actually depends on your determination and patience. You have it within your psyche to exercise this function of imagination and to use it actively. This opens you up to an experience of the inner world and a connection to the unconscious.

As well as following the rules, it's also important not to interpret the active imagination while it is happening. Just let it unfold and record it. Understanding the meaning will come later, but meanwhile don't use your cognitive functions of interpretation, or it will block further development. Active imagination is an experience of image, story, and feeling. You'll find that you can become very emotional while doing active imagination. That's why it's wise to put a time limit on it; 20 or 30 minutes a day is really enough. Don't get overly involved, and always keep conscious control over this imaginative activity in which you're engaging.

In experimenting with active imagination, you should write down everything that you experience, see, hear, or feel. Be sure to include it in your journal, because you want to be able to go back and trace your steps later. Do not be tempted to interpret too much as you go. Wait until the process has been very well established before looking into the meaning. Just stay with the symbols and figures and keep working with them. When the series has run its course, you can try to interpret it using suitable psychological concepts.

References

Abramovitch, H. (2021). "When Is It Time to Stop? When Good Enough Becomes Bad Enough." *Journal of Analytical Psychology* 66:4.

Corbin, H. (1972). "*Mundus Imaginalis* or The Imaginary and the Imaginal." Spring 1972, pp. 1-33.

Ellenberger, H. (1970). *The Discovery of the Unconscious: The History and Evolution of Dynamic Psychiatry*. New York: Basic Books.

Jacoby, M. (1984). *The Analytic Encounter: Transference and Human Relationship*. Toronto: Inner City Books.

_____. (1985). *Longing for Paradise*. Boston: Sigo Press.

Jung, C.G. (1916/1969). "The Transcendent Function." *Collected Works*, vol. 8.

_____. (1931/1966). "Problems of Modern Psychotherapy." *Collected Works*, vol. 16.

_____. (1938/1969). "The Stages of Life." *Collected Works*, vol. 8.

_____. (1950/1968). "A Study in the Process of Individuation," *Collected Works*, vol. 9i.

____. (1961). *Memories, Dreams, Reflections*. New York: Vintage Books.

____. (1968). "Psychology and Alchemy." *Collected Works*, vol. 12.

____. (1997). *Visions: Notes of the Seminar Given in 1930-1934*. 2 volumes. Claire Douglas (ed.). Princeton, NJ: Princeton University Press.

____. (2009) *The Red Book: Liber Novus*. New York: W.W. Norton & Co.

McGuire, W. (1974). *The Freud/Jung Letters*. Princeton, NJ: Princeton University Press.

Neumann, E. (1954). *The Origins and History of Consciousness*. Princeton, NJ: Princeton University Press.

Wheelwright, J. (1982). "Termination." M. Stein (ed.), *Jungian Analysis*. Chicago: Open Court.

CPSIA information can be obtained
at www.ICGtesting.com
Printed in the USA
LVHW050445110222
710793LV00004B/189

9 781685 030254